THIRTY WOODEN BOATS

A SECOND CATALOG OF BUILDING PLANS

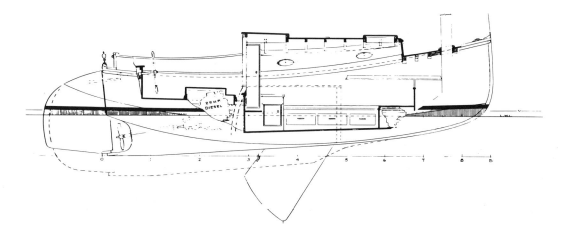

By The Editors
of
WoodenBoat Magazine

Published by WoodenBoat Publications, Inc.
Naskeag Road
Brooklin, Maine 04616

Library of Congress Cataloging-in-Publication Data

Thirty wooden boats: a second catalog of building plans / by the
  editors of WoodenBoat magazine.
        p.   cm.
  Bibliography: p.
  ISBN 0–937822–15–9 : $8.95
    1. Boats and boating—Designs and plans—Catalogs.
  I. Woodenboat. II. Title: 30 wooden boats.
VM321.T47   1987
623.8'2023—dc 19   88–20586
                                                         CIP

A Catalog of Building Plans

WoodenBoat

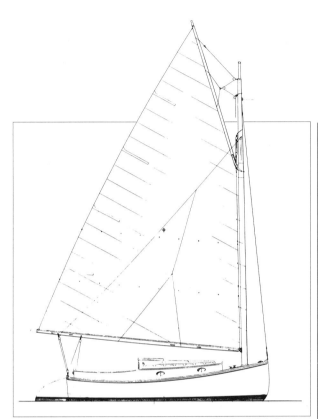

20' Plywood Catboat, Madam Tirza, by Charles Wittholz

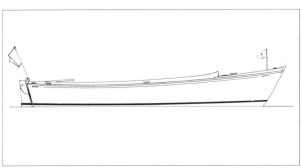

18'7" Utility Launch, Barbara Anne, by Robert M. Steward

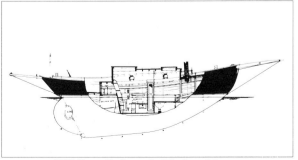

24'6" Sloop Typhoon, by Winthrop Warner

Introduction

This is our second substantial catalog of study plans for wooden boats. Our first, *Fifty Wooden Boats*, which was published in 1984, has proven to be a wonderful tool for learning about and understanding the varieties of wooden boats. Such catalogs as these are at once food for thought and fuel for dreams. And at their best, they provide us with opportunities to compare varieties of hull and rig, and to consider how interior arrangements fit with our own ideals for accommodation. We can compare a classic runabout with a contemporary launch, we can compare canoes, daysailers, and small cruising boats, and we can be inspired by the possibilities they all offer.

In our ongoing search for designs suitable for both amateur and professional construction, we have attempted to select for simplicity, utility, beauty, and ease of construction. In some cases, these are conflicting objectives, which makes the process both challenging and engaging. Some of these designs have been commissioned by WoodenBoat, in order to meet particular needs in distinctive ways. Others have been included as much for their ability to educate and inform students of yacht and boat design.

There are many fine designers whose works are not represented in this collection, and more fine designs than we can ever hope to include in future collections. We have selected or commissioned the plans included here because we believe they should be more widely available. As agents for the designers whose works are included, we have a responsibility to encourage good workmanship in every respect. To that end, the research and technical departments at WoodenBoat remain ready to assist builders with answers to questions and references to further readings.

The descriptive data and essays on each boat, combined with the general material on boat design and the extensive bibliography, make this a highly useful resource. Cynthia Curtis, Mike O'Brien, and Paul Lazarus, its compilers, have endeavored to provide readers with as much information as possible while maintaining an open and strongly visual format. Our hope is that it is both informative and inspiring, and that you will find much that is useful in these pages.

Jon Wilson, Editor
WoodenBoat magazine

Looking at Boat Plans

Text and drawings by Joel White

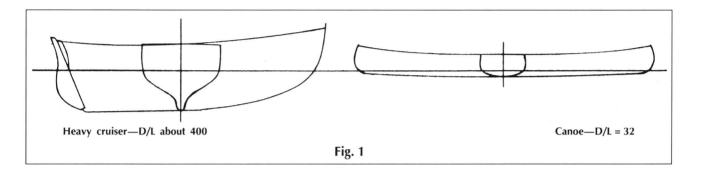

Heavy cruiser—D/L about 400   Canoe—D/L = 32

Fig. 1

The interpretation of plans takes time and experience; a lifetime of studying boats helps. But the basic knowledge needed is pretty simple, and a passion for boats and boat design will carry one a long way down the path of understanding. Let's think a bit about the basics.

Displacement and Displacement/Length Ratio

Archimedes decided a long time ago that anything floating in water displaces a volume of water which will equal the weight of the floating object. I'm glad he came up with this notion, as it makes naval architecture simple enough that even my arithmetic can handle most situations. A calculation of the volume in cubic feet of a boat's hull below its floating waterline multiplied by the density of the liquid in which it is floating—64 lbs per cu ft for salt water—will give the weight of the displaced liquid, and, as Archimedes pointed out, this always equals the weight of the object (boat). So—a boat displacing 10 cu ft (the volume of the hull below the waterline) would weigh 640 lbs when floating in the ocean. If you weigh 192 lbs and step into the boat, it will immediately sink into the water until it displaces an additional 3 cu ft (192 ÷ 64), for a total of 13 cu ft.

Simply knowing the displacement, or weight, of a particular boat is only marginally useful in evaluating a design. What you need is a method of comparison; you need to know whether it is an ultralight or a heavyweight, or something in between. Someone who came along after Archimedes figured out that a nondimensional ratio between length and displacement would be a useful tool for comparing boats of differing sizes and types. We calculate this so-called displacement/length ratio (D/L) as follows: D/L Ratio = D + (.01L)³, or D/(L/100)³, where D = displacement in long tons of 2,240 lbs, and L = waterline length in feet. (The .01 is there to make the resulting number fall in the 1–500 range so it is easier to deal with; the length must be cubed in order to make the ratio nondimensional, and thus be useful for comparing boats of widely varying size.) The displacement/length ratio of most boats works out to between 50 and 400: under 100 is considered superlight; 100–200, light; 200–300, medium;

300–400, heavy. For ratios over 400, the boat is a real chunk.

Figure 1 shows two boats at opposite ends of the displacement/length scale: a heavy cruiser at D/L = 400, and a canoe at D/L = 32.

Perhaps I can make this concept easier to visualize by using a canoe as an example. Suppose you own a canoe with a 15′ waterline, weighing 50 lbs. Let's calculate the displacement/length ratio for three different loadings: A—empty; B—192-lb person aboard; C—four people and some camping gear, which total 900 lbs.

Figure 2 shows that the heavily loaded canoe (overloaded, really) with you, three friends, and your tent,

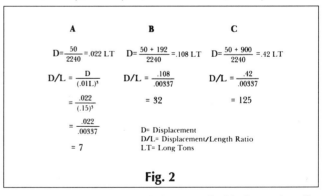

Fig. 2

A

$$D = \frac{50}{2240} = .022 \text{ LT}$$

$$D/L = \frac{D}{(.01L)^3}$$

$$= \frac{.022}{(.15)^3}$$

$$= \frac{.022}{.00337}$$

$$= 7$$

B

$$D = \frac{50 + 192}{2240} = .108 \text{ LT}$$

$$D/L = \frac{.108}{.00337}$$

$$= 32$$

C

$$D = \frac{50 + 900}{2240} = .42 \text{ LT}$$

$$D/L = \frac{.42}{.00337}$$

$$= 125$$

D = Displacement
D/L = Displacement/Length Ratio
LT = Long Tons

food, clothes, and bedrolls has nearly 20 times the displacement/length ratio of the unloaded canoe. If you have done any canoeing, you know that the loaded canoe is much steadier in the water than the light one, that it takes much more effort to propel, and that it bounces around much less in a chop. Similar changes take place in sailboats or powerboats as displacement/length ratios increase. Although some designers are reluctant to publish lines plans, most will give waterline length and displacement figures, and by using only these two numbers, you can quickly calculate into which weight category the design falls and make some early judgments as to its

This article reprinted from WoodenBoat No. 75

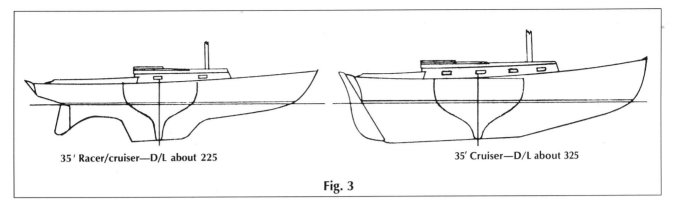

35' Racer/cruiser—D/L about 225   35' Cruiser—D/L about 325

Fig. 3

characteristics. If its displacement/length ratio is 100—and it has enough sail area—it should be fast and lively; because of this, it is likely to be wet, particularly going to windward. If the displacement/length ratio is 300, the boat will be steadier, slower unless very heavily canvased, and probably more seaworthy and less scary under difficult conditions. If the two boats are the same length, the heavier boat will have more room for accommodations, which puts it into the cruiser category. The light boat will have more spartan and lighter-weight accommodations, and would probably be classified as a racing or racing-cruiser type. So the D/L ratio is a good indication of a boat's characteristics and abilities.

Figure 3 shows two 35-footers: the first, a racer-cruiser type with D/L = 225; the second, a pure cruiser, with D/L = 325.

Balance

Always a mystery area, the balance of a sailing boat—how it steers, whether or not it has weather helm—is of serious concern to the designer. Balance cannot be calculated with the same precision as displacement can, and so the naval architect often worries whether a new design will balance correctly. A slight tendency to head into the wind, offset by a few degrees of helm, is considered ideal. The weather helm usually increases as the wind breezes up and the boat heels, and it is easy to understand why: If you visualize a heeled sailboat as viewed from a helicopter hovering directly overhead, the center of effort (CE) of the sail plan will move off to leeward of the hull more and more as the boat heels further. The CE of the sail plan is where the driving force of the wind is centered. The resistance, or drag of the hull, on the other hand, is offset to windward as the hull heels. Because these two opposing forces (the wind trying to move the boat ahead, while the drag tries to resist) are not above one another, a strong twisting action is created which tries to turn the boat into the wind. This so-called turning moment is offset only by the tiller being pulled to windward. Figure 4 illustrates what happens when a boat heels.

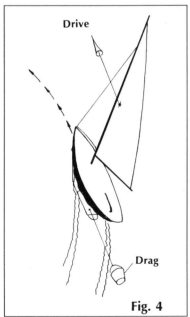

Drive

Drag

Fig. 4

When the sail plan of a new design is drawn, the designer calculates the center of area of each sail, and combines these individual centers into an overall center of area, or center of effort (CE), for the entire sail plan. He also plots the fore-and-aft center of area of the boat's underwater profile (usually counting only one-half the area of the rudder), determines its geometric center, and labels this the center of lateral resistance, or CLR. The relationship between the CE and the CLR—that is, the horizontal distance between them expressed as a percentage of the waterline length—is termed the "lead." It has been found by trial and error that, as a general rule, the CE should lie forward of the CLR by 10–20% of the waterline length to produce a well-balanced vessel. Increasing the amount of lead, by moving either the CE of the sail plan forward or moving the CLR aft, will help to reduce the weather helm. If the lead is too great, lee helm can be the result, a condition that should always be avoided.

Figure 5 shows the lead on a small sloop.

There can be considerable variation in leads—gaff schooners often have much less, modern fin-keeled designs with tall rigs sometimes have more. Each designer checks a new boat's balance during trials to learn how his latest guess as to lead has panned out. Hull shape also affects the amount of lead. As boats heel, the shape of the hull underwater becomes assymetrical about the center-

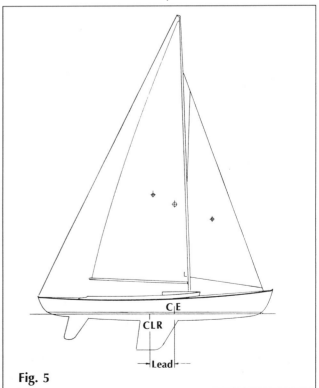

CE

CLR

Lead

Fig. 5

line; beamy boats are particularly inclined to do this. The diagram below (Figure 6) illustrates a wide catboat underbody when heeled to 18°. As you can see, the shape becomes such that the hull will have a strong tendency to turn to windward. This, added to the turning couple shown in Figure 4, explains why some beamy boats have an almost unmanageable weather helm and why designers become prematurely gray.

So, when examining a new design, see if the designer

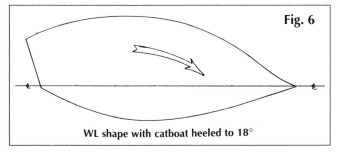

Fig. 6

WL shape with catboat heeled to 18°

marked the CE and CLR on the drawings (usually the sail plan)—if he didn't, you can work it out yourself—and notice the amount of lead. If it doesn't fall in the 10–20% range, wonder why.

Steadiness and Maneuverability

Let's think about how the shape of the underwater profile affects a boat's other steering and handling qualities. A sailboat with a deep forefoot and a long, straight keel running aft to a moderately raked or vertical rudderpost will have a great deal of underwater profile area (to resist leeway) and a lot of wetted surface, and will be slow to turn because of having to twist all this profile area sideways through the water. She almost surely will be slow in stays (coming about), and the large wetted surface may make her a slow sailer, unless offset by a large sail area. The same boat in a heavy sea, for the same reasons, will not be thrown about as violently, and will steer a steadier course as compared with a boat with a small underwater profile—a modern fin-keeled boat, perhaps, with the underwater ends cut away, and a separate rudder aft. This same fin-keeler will be quick in stays, probably faster, but more fidgety in a seaway, and will require more attention and concentration from her helmsman. As in life itself, boats demand compromise, and to gain quickness in stays you must give up some steadiness in a seaway. The trend today is toward cutaway underbodies, fin keels, and lighter displacement. The resulting boats are swift, nervous, and if carried to extremes, sometimes dangerous offshore.

Seaworthiness

There is a great deal of interest in what makes a boat seaworthy, and rightly so. Nobody wants to set sail for Bermuda in a boat that is not capable of handling the sea conditions likely to be met during the voyage. There is also a great deal of misconception about what makes a boat seaworthy. Many people believe it is all a matter of hull shape, but this plays only a small part. Seaworthiness is the sum of all the factors which make a boat able to remain at sea and survive about anything that comes along. The hull must be strong and tight, the deck structures must be able to withstand the pounding of boarding seas, and the deck openings must be located so that the boat cannot be flooded, even in a knockdown. The rig must be strong against failure in severe weather conditions, and even survive knockdowns and rollovers, God forbid. The ballast must be secured so that it cannot shift

under any circumstances. The crew must be experienced enough to handle the boat correctly in bad weather, and be able to navigate as well. A deepwater passagemaker may conform to all the conditions above except one, and that one weak link may do her in. So, seaworthiness is a condition brought about by combining many strong features into a strong whole, and cannot be conjured up simply by a designer drawing the right lines on paper.

However, let's discuss seaworthiness only as it applies to hull design. I don't think it is always correct to say that one hull shape is seaworthy and another is not. I do think there are certain basic characteristics which contribute to a good seaboat. Having balanced ends is one—a boat that is full forward should also be full aft. If she is fine forward, she should not have a large, full stern. A full stern in such a boat, when running off before large seas, may be lifted due to its excessive buoyancy and force the fine bow underwater, causing the boat to trip or broach.

A good seaboat needs a certain amount of freeboard for reserve buoyancy so the decks aren't continually swept by seas, but not so much freeboard that she is lacking in stability (through a too-high center of gravity) or has too much windage. And, of course, her stability is very important—her ability to recover from 90°-or-greater knockdowns. We will cover stability in more detail in the next section.

The speed at which a boat is driven in a heavy sea has much effect on her motion—the faster she goes, the bumpier the ride, and the more chance for a broach. A boat traveling at high speed under press of sail in a severe storm may be unseaworthy, while the same vessel, hove to or slowly running off, will ride the seas like a duck. Many people have been sold the idea that the Colin Archer type of double-ender is the ultimate seaboat, but my feeling is that boats like this do well in rough water only because most of them are inherently slow to windward and therefore unable to get into much trouble.

I do think that most very lightweight boats are less seaworthy than their heavier sisters—but not because of shape or lightness, per se. By their nature, they have to have lighter construction scantlings than do medium-weight cruisers—they have to, in order to keep the displacement to the designed weight—so generally their structural members are designed to a lower factor of safety in order that the boat will float on her lines while carrying enough ballast to be stable. Modern construction methods have done much to improve these safety factors, but things are still more likely to break in craft of very light displacement. And these same ultralights have a more violent motion in bad weather than do the heavier cruisers. Remember how the displacement/length ratio affected our canoe? This snapping and jerking motion not only can damage the rig or hull structure, it can tire the crew and lessen their ability to handle the boat.

Well, you say, he still hasn't told us what shape the hull should be for seaworthiness. I am not sure that I can. Most strongly built boats with balanced ends and neither too much nor too little freeboard, a displacement/length ratio of 200 or more, manned by a strong, smart crew, can survive almost any storm. Notice the "almost." I don't believe that there is such a thing as a small boat that can survive every storm. The waterfront news still contains an occasional story of the disappearance at sea of what seemed to be a well-found and well-crewed vessel. I think it will always be so—rare but unavoidable. The odds of this happening can be made very small, but cannot be reduced to zero.

Continued on page 70

12' Wee Rob Canoe

by Iain Oughtred

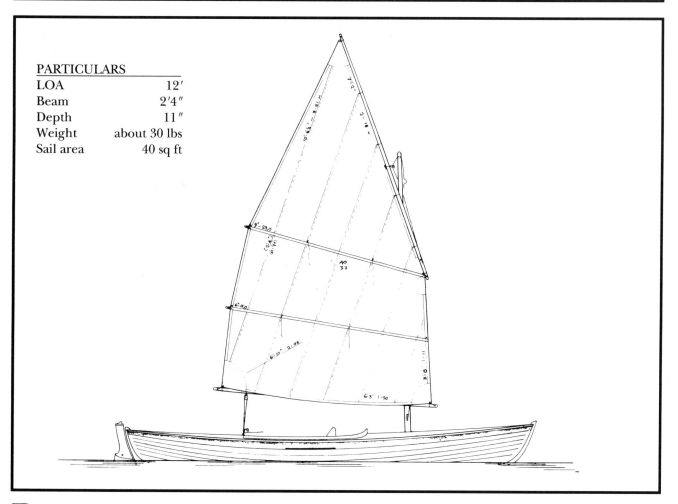

PARTICULARS

LOA	12'
Beam	2'4"
Depth	11"
Weight	about 30 lbs
Sail area	40 sq ft

Recreational canoeing began in Britain and America in the latter half of the 19th century in boats similar to Iain Oughtred's Wee Rob. The general type came to be known as the Rob Roy canoe, after a popular, archetypal vessel by that name. Oughtred's 12-footer—being a small version of the original breed—is named accordingly.

In recent years there has been a revival of double-paddle sailing canoes, as more people rediscover the versatility of these lovely craft. Traditional construction, though, of what is essentially a tiny yacht can be a challenging project—given light scantlings, solid lumber, tight spaces, and a complex round-bottomed shape. Wee Rob can certainly be built in the traditional manner, and Oughtred has specified information for that option. However, the real purpose and appeal of this design (as with much of Iain Oughtred's work) is to facilitate rather than complicate construction, so the builder can go boating in a traditional craft after a minimum of shop time.

To that end, Wee Rob requires no lofting, because patterns are provided for the stems and the station molds. Also, the preferred building method here is glued-seam lapstrake plywood construction, which requires few fastenings and no internal framing, and for which sheet materials are readily available in marine grades. More-over, the designer has predetermined the plank shapes and prepared an illustrated, instructional monograph for building small boats by this system.

The construction drawing in the plans set shows not only the Wee Rob's building jig but—along with the sail plan—a variety of auxiliary parts and appurtenances should the builder elect to produce a decked rather than open canoe, or create a lug-rigged leeboard sailer of the basic double-paddler.

Finally, provisions have been made and revised patterns furnished for lengthened versions (at 13'7" or 15'2") of this hull on the same beam.

The standard model of a Wee Rob would be as handy a singlehander and cartop cruiser as you're likely to find. And to find one, friends, is to build one, since boats like this are not seen at the store; but she's well worth the effort. Wee Rob offers the opportunity to do some old-time, commemorative canoeing: a return to the roots of recreational small craft, in a modern boat.

The plans consist of five sheets which include lines and offsets, construction and sail plans, plus patterns for molds and stems that are marked for plank lands. Also included are a materials list and the designer's 14-page building booklet. WB Plan No. 79. $50.00.

Plan 79

DESCRIPTION
Hull type: Round-bottomed canoe
Rig: Single lug
Construction: Glued lapstrake plywood

PERFORMANCE
*Suitable for: Protected waters
*Intended capacity: 1
 Trailerable: Cartop

See page 78 for further information.

Propulsion: Double paddle, sail
Speed (knots): 2–4

BUILDING DATA
Skill needed: Basic to intermediate
Lofting required: No
*Alternative construction: Traditional lapstrake,
    cold-molded, strip

PLANS DATA
No. of sheets: 5 plus instruction booklet
Level of detail: Above average
Cost per set: $50.00
WB Plan No. 79

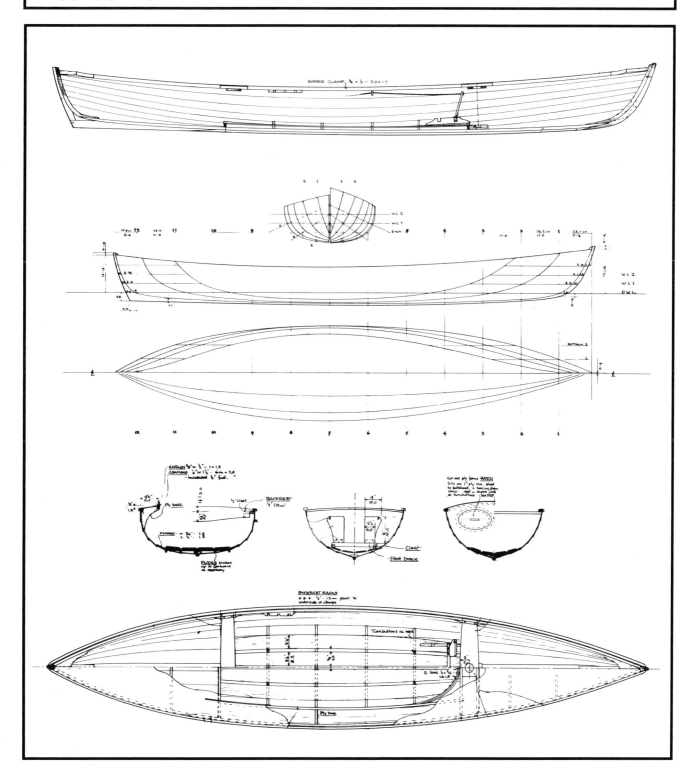

13'7" MacGregor Canoe

by Iain Oughtred

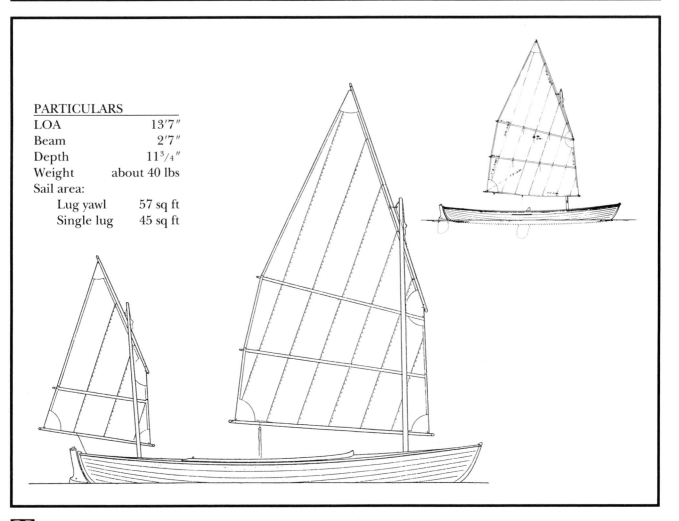

PARTICULARS

LOA	13'7"
Beam	2'7"
Depth	11¾"
Weight	about 40 lbs
Sail area:	
Lug yawl	57 sq ft
Single lug	45 sq ft

The 19th-century Scot, John MacGregor, is generally credited with devising the decked, double-paddle sailing canoe, then popularizing it by writing of international cruises he made aboard his canoe ROB ROY.

The Iain Oughtred design presented here is the larger of two Oughtred-designed canoes offered by Wooden-Boat, although at 13'7" it is a bit smaller than many first-generation boats of this type.

But unlike the original models, Oughtred's Mac-Gregor can be built on a tight schedule and with average skills, thanks to the recent development of glued-seam lapstrake plywood construction. To further ease and accelerate the building process, Oughtred has provided lofting-free full-sized patterns, predetermined plank shapes, highly detailed plans, and a companion instructional booklet on methods and materials.

The MacGregor shares much with her smaller sister, Wee Rob (WB Plan No. 79). Both are ultralight, traditionally attractive, versatile canoes. Both offer decked/undecked options; both can be expanded to longer lengths on a fixed beam; and both have been given the seakeeping benefits of greater flare, freeboard, and keel rocker than were typical of the old canoes of this kind.

A further refinement in Oughtred's design is the marked reduction of excesses in joinerwork and rigging often seen in the older boats. A simple bulkhead opening has replaced deck hatches; a quick-change leeboard replaces a complex, folding centerboard; and simplified (but still authentic) sail plans—a single lug or a battened lug yawl—eliminate a snarl of "strings" to pull.

Early double-paddle canoes were classified according to their order of abilities (paddle, sail, cruise, race); Oughtred's pair of canoes follows that convention. Given her longer waterline length and larger sail plan, the MacGregor is more of a sailer than her sister, but each of these canoes will perform capably with double paddle or sail, and as cruising, rather than racing craft.

The designer has specified scantlings for those who prefer conventional, plank-on-frame, lapstrake construction (see WB Nos. 36 and 37); he has also provided offsets and stem patterns for building this boat at 15'8" or 17'3".

There are five sheets of plans containing lines and offsets, construction, two sail plans, plus mold and stem patterns showing plank lands. Additional items include a comprehensive materials list, and the 14-page illustrated text on building procedures. WB Plan No. 80. $60.00.

Plan 80

DESCRIPTION
Hull type: Round-bottomed canoe
Rig: Lug yawl or single lug
Construction: Glued lapstrake plywood

PERFORMANCE
*Suitable for: Protected waters
*Intended capacity: 1–2
Trailerable: Cartop

See page 78 for further information.

Propulsion: Sail, double paddle
Speed (knots): 2–4

BUILDING DATA
Skill needed: Basic to intermediate
Lofting required: No
*Alternative construction: Traditional lapstrake, cold-molded, strip

PLANS DATA
No. of sheets: 5 plus instruction booklet
Level of detail: Above average
Cost per set: $60.00
WB Plan No. 80

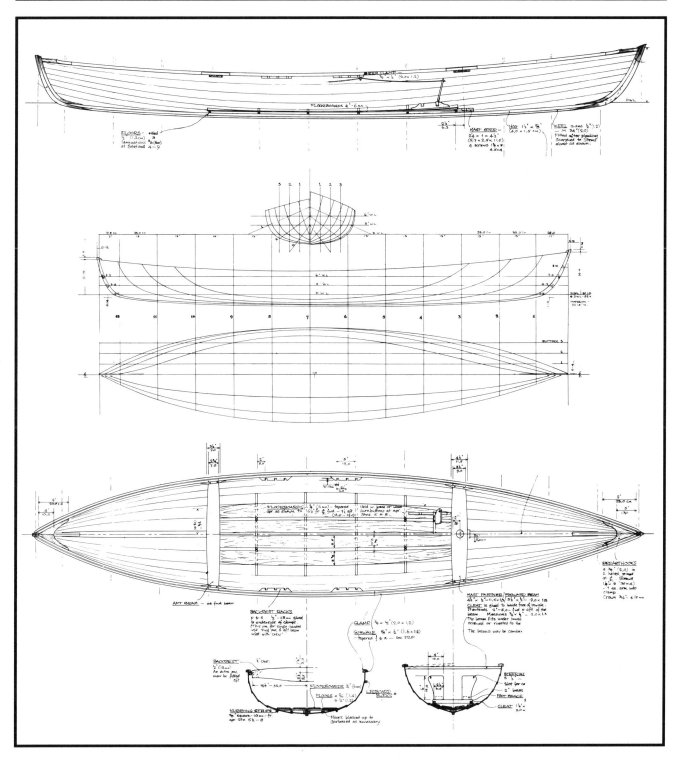

15′ Sea Kayak, Tursiops

by Michael B. Alford

PARTICULARS

LOA	15′
Beam	2′4″
Weight	about 42 lbs

Drawn by a professional designer for his own use, Tursiops is a most personal and versatile craft. Properly handled, she can cross incredibly wild water, find a placid pond, and leave the tranquility untouched.

She's wide at her rail (28″)—most American touring kayaks carry about 24″, and many British boats are 22″ or less. This relatively great beam takes little from her top speed and practically nothing from her touring pace, but it makes Eskimo rolling more difficult. The point is that she won't capsize easily—and if she does go over, "wet rescues" will be easier than for narrow boats. In any case, her beam and nicely shaped ends give her gentle manners—there's no treachery in this kayak.

Designer Mike Alford describes the criteria that led to Tursiops' creation: "My goal was to get across four or five miles of open water from the mainland to a string of uninhabited barrier islands. I needed to carry a fair amount of camera gear and a day's rations. Any number of boats might seem satisfactory for this purpose, but the catch was that I didn't want to stake a boat out or worry about tide stranding, vandalism, or motor theft. A sea kayak offered all the mobility and rough-water survivability called for, and had the advantage that it could stow unobtrusively under a bush."

Tursiops' graceful lines belie her simple construction—she has one of the prettiest sheet-plywood hulls we've seen. Alford has done a nice job of working the transition from the peaked foredeck to the flat (for securing gear) afterdeck—often an awkward area in similar designs.

This friendly kayak might be a nearly perfect "impulse boat." She'll ride happily on top of your car waiting to explore a stream running unnoticed under a highway bridge, and she'll tackle open water with equal enthusiasm.

Four sheets of drawings show lines, offsets, construction, profile and deck arrangement, and include patterns and templates. WB Plan No. 85. $45.00.

Plan 85

DESCRIPTION
Hull type: V-bottomed
Construction: Plywood over web frames
PERFORMANCE
*Suitable for: Protected waters
*Intended capacity: 1
 Trailerable: Cartop

See page 78 for further information.

Propulsion: Double-paddle
Speed (knots): 4–5 $\frac{1}{2}$
BUILDING DATA
Skill needed: Basic to intermediate
Lofting required: Yes
*Alternative construction: None
PLANS DATA
No. of sheets: 4
Level of detail: Above average
Cost per set: $45.00
WB Plan No. 85

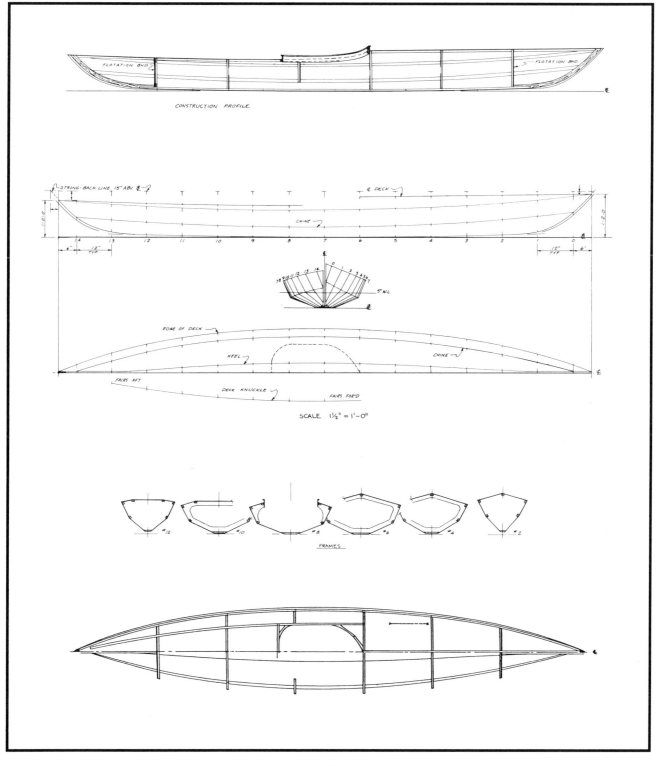

CONSTRUCTION PROFILE

SCALE 1½" = 1'-0"

FRAMES

7'10" Acorn Tender

by Iain Oughtred

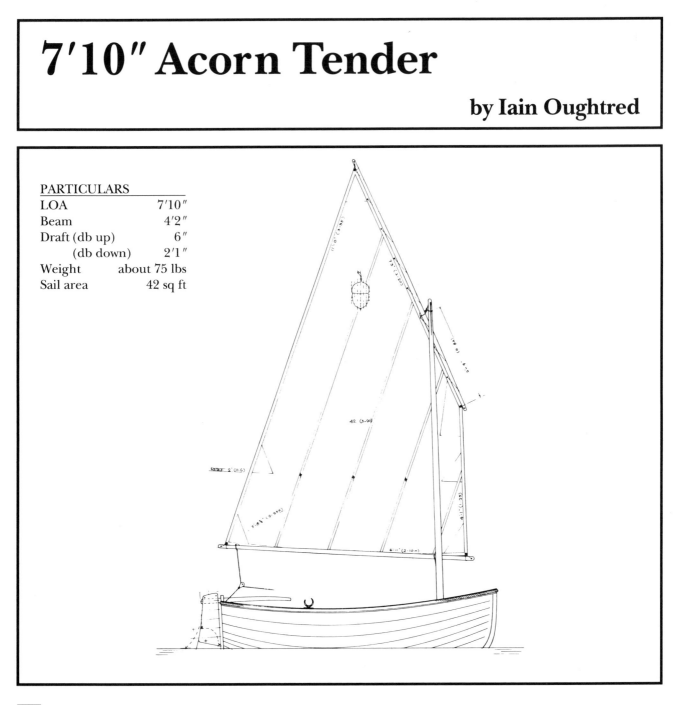

PARTICULARS

LOA	7'10"
Beam	4'2"
Draft (db up)	6"
(db down)	2'1"
Weight	about 75 lbs
Sail area	42 sq ft

This sweet-lined tender is the smallest in Iain Oughtred's design series of Acorn skiffs and dinghies. She is sufficiently burdensome to be useful as a general-purpose shuttle from ship to shore; she is also handsome and light enough to be carried on deck or in davits aboard the mother yacht. And what is more, her overall length can be shortened to suit—from 7'10" to 7'7" or 7'5", as needed and as per plans.

Like other Oughtred design offerings, the Acorn tender may be built traditionally of solid lumber to heavier specifications. But the preferred and featured building method here is frameless, glued-seam, lapstrake plywood construction—an excellent system for amateurs in particular, and an efficient procedure for lapstrake small craft in general. The dimensionally stable plywood allows boats to be kept ashore for long periods without drying out, and the frameless interior makes maintenance easier.

Consistent, too, with his other designs, Oughtred's tender allows for multiple choices in other areas. This boat may be set up for sail with either a standing- or balanced-lug rig, a leeboard or daggerboard, and a fixed or pivoting rudder; or she can be outfitted for oars and outboard only.

The Acorn 8 can be constructed without lofting, using standard sheets of marine plywood. She can be finished plain or fancy, according to taste and role requirements. There is no keen technical skill required, since all the necessary information from building the jig and constructing the hull to the final fitting out, is contained in Oughtred's packet of plans.

This packet consists of four sheets: lines, construction, sail, and full-sized patterns for plank lands and major parts. Included as well are detailed construction notes, a tools list and materials schedule, and a 14-page booklet illustrating the plywood building procedure. There are also recommendations and data regarding conventional construction. WB Plan No. 87. $55.00.

Plan 87

DESCRIPTION
Hull type: Round-bottomed
Rig: Standing lug sail
Construction: Glued lapstrake plywood
PERFORMANCE
~~Suitable for~~ protected waters
*~~Intended~~
~~Trailerable~~

~~See text for further information.~~

Propulsion: Sail, oars, outboard
Speed (knots): 3
BUILDING DATA
Skill needed: Basic to intermediate
Lofting required: No
*Alternative construction: Traditional lapstrake
PLANS DATA
No. of sheets: 4 plus instruction booklet
Level of detail: Above average
Cost per set: $55.00
WB Plan No. 87

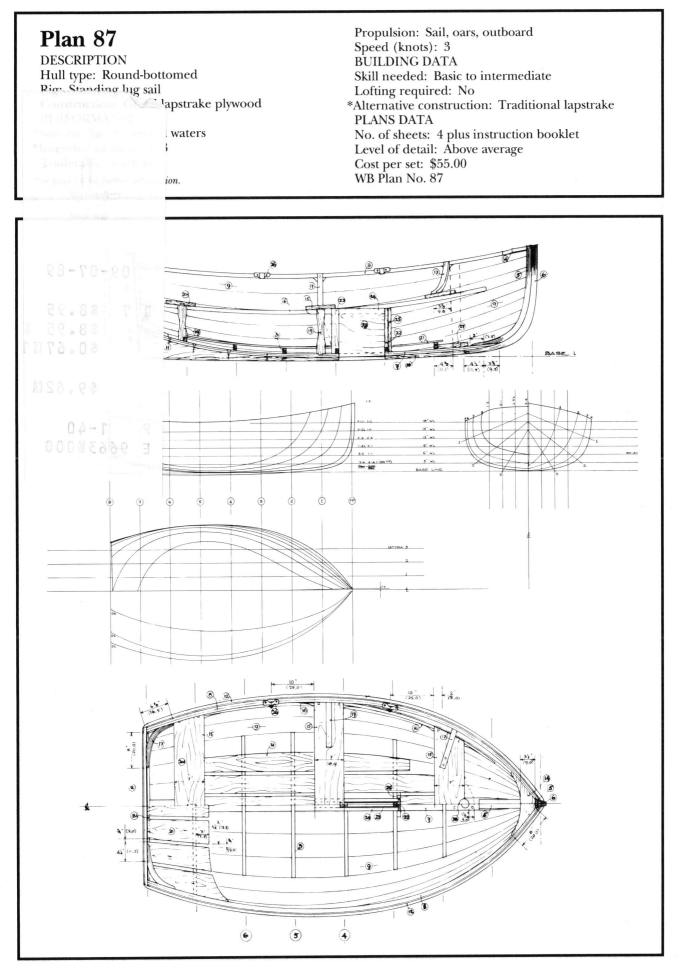

10'2" Acorn Dinghy

by Iain Oughtred

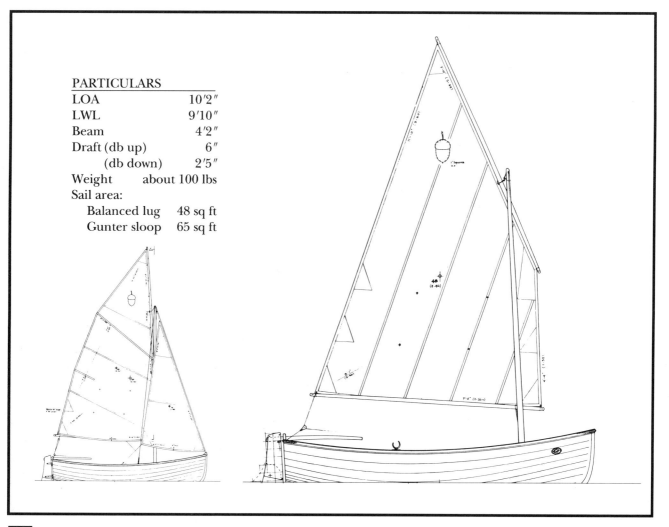

PARTICULARS

LOA	10'2"
LWL	9'10"
Beam	4'2"
Draft (db up)	6"
(db down)	2'5"
Weight	about 100 lbs
Sail area:	
Balanced lug	48 sq ft
Gunter sloop	65 sq ft

The Acorn 10-footer by Iain Oughtred is intermediate in size and shape between his longer skiff (WB Plan No. 43) and his shorter tender (WB Plan No. 87). She is a dinghy designed for seaworthy service and multiple use—in tow behind a yacht, in harbor as a lighter, and in protected waters as a lugger. Alternatively, she can be rigged for added performance under sail, or simply employed as a businesslike utility under oars or outboard power.

Her type is that of a traditional ship's boat—beamy and burdensome, with good stability and carrying capacity for her length, and a hull that is easily driven if properly handled and trimmed. She is an all-around craft, as versatile a vessel as can be found in this difficult-to-design size range.

Oughtred has not only achieved a good-looking, multi-purpose small-boat design, he has done a great deal to relieve the builder of the difficulty commonly associated with round-bottomed lapstrake construction. And he has managed this in his usual manner: by producing a very comprehensive set of plans (lofting is not required), and by selecting a building system that lends itself to amateur construction.

The building method—glued-seam lapstrake plywood—is further enhanced by a frameless interior that permits faster assembly, reduced maintenance, and adjustable thwart locations.

The basic single-sail rig for the Acorn 10 can be a balanced or standing lug—either one being an easy and efficient sail plan to set up, stow, and operate. A second, enlarged sail plan calls for a gunter-rigged sloop, thereby converting this dinghy into a lively sailer and enabling it to serve as an excellent graduated trainer through the various levels of small-boat handling and seamanship.

Choices within the sailing options include leeboard, daggerboard, or centerboard, and a fixed or pivoting rudder. Gunwale and transom choices are also presented in the plans, as are general data and scantlings for those wishing to construct this boat traditionally of solid wood.

The plans packet contains: five sheets of drawings—lines, construction, full-sized patterns, lug and sloop rigs; materials list; construction notes for both modern and traditional methods; and a booklet illustrating the plywood building procedure for the Acorn boats. WB Plan No. 88. $60.00.

Plan 88

DESCRIPTION
Hull type: Round-bottomed
Rig: Balanced lug or gunter sloop
Construction: Glued lapstrake plywood
PERFORMANCE
*Suitable for: Protected waters
*Intended capacity: 2–3
 Trailerable: Cartop

See page 78 for further information.

Propulsion: Sail, oars, outboard
Speed (knots): 3
BUILDING DATA
Skill needed: Basic to intermediate
Lofting required: No
*Alternative construction: Traditional lapstrake
PLANS DATA
No. of sheets: 5 plus instruction booklet
Level of detail: Above average
Cost per set: $60.00
WB Plan No. 88

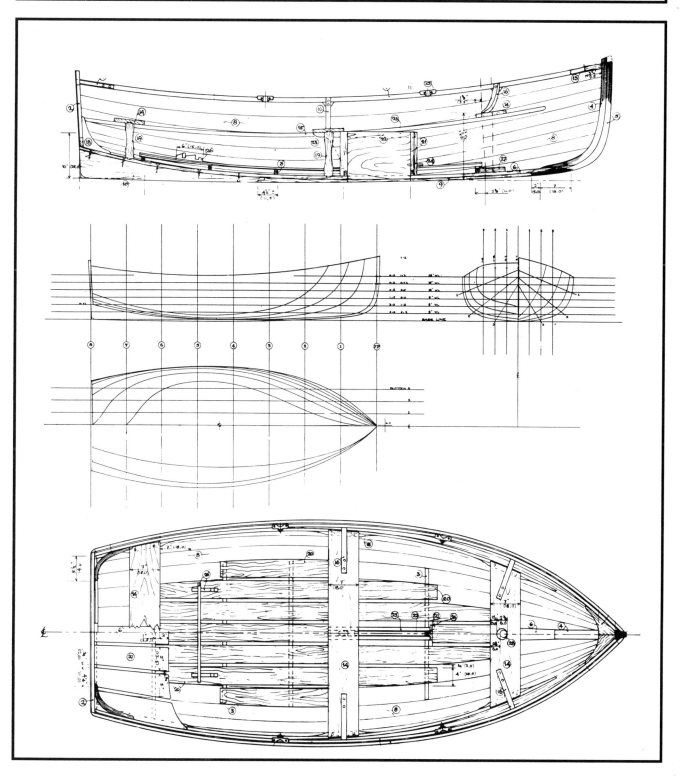

15'8" Stickleback Dory

by Iain Oughtred

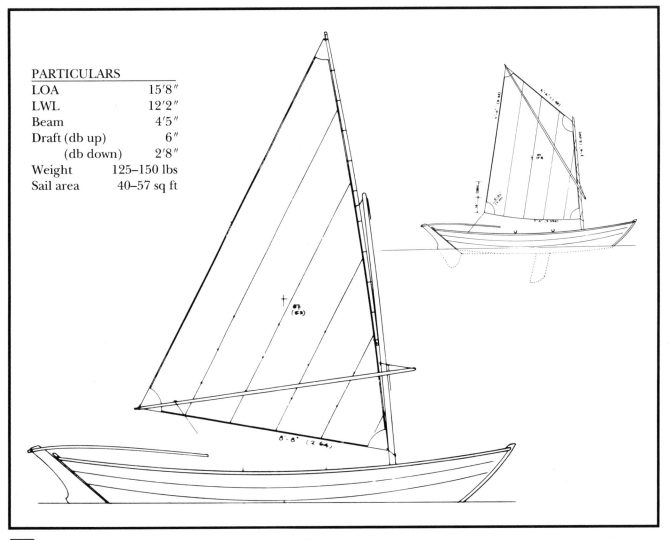

PARTICULARS

LOA	15'8"
LWL	12'2"
Beam	4'5"
Draft (db up)	6"
(db down)	2'8"
Weight	125–150 lbs
Sail area	40–57 sq ft

The stickleback—a rather rakish anadromous fish whose life cycle involves both fresh and salt water—seems an apt choice of names for this fine design by Iain Oughtred. Here is a long and lean rowing-and-sailing machine which, at less than 16' overall, is a smaller, lighter, and handier version of his 18' John Dory (WB Plan No. 81).

Like her larger sister, this boat is a Swampscott—a very successful and shapely type among the various generic dory designs. The knuckle-sided hull gives her the performance characteristics of a round-bottomed craft, yet, at the same time, her flat bottom affords easier beaching and, in conjunction with the sawn frames, faster construction.

With the glued-seam, lapstrake-plywood construction preferred by Oughtred, his Stickleback weighs significantly less than the same boat built traditionally of solid lumber, though scantlings are provided for that option.

This dory can be finished out as either a light- or moderate-duty workboat (Swampscotts, as a breed, began as commercial fishing craft), including a built-in well for

a small outboard motor. Or she can be dressed out in a number of recreational setups that enable the builder to mix and match, including: open or partially decked rowing or sailing layouts with or without the buoyancy and dry stowage of watertight compartments; and three different sail plans (one sprit and two gunter rigs) along with either a rigid or lifting rudder and daggerboard. There are, as with all of Oughtred's work, additional minor modifications of parts and rigging indicated on the plans, allowing ample opportunity for customizing.

The building sequence for Oughtred's dories is illustrated in a step-by-step booklet using drawings for the plywood hull construction, and photographs for the numerous details involved in completion and fitting out. Full-sized patterns for the plank lands and hull structure eliminate the lofting process.

The Stickleback plans are on four sheets: lines and sail plans, construction, and full-sized patterns. Included in the plans set are a materials schedule, construction notes, and the dory-building booklet described above. WB Plan No. 86. $60.00.

Plan 86

DESCRIPTION
Hull type: Flat-bottomed, round-sided dory
Rig: Sprit or gunter
Construction: Glued lapstrake plywood over
  sawn frames
PERFORMANCE
*Suitable for: Protected waters
*Intended capacity: 2–4
  Trailerable: Yes

See page 78 for further information.

Propulsion: Sail, oars, outboard
Speed (knots): 2–4
BUILDING DATA
Skill needed: Basic to intermediate
Lofting required: No
*Alternative construction: Traditional dory
  construction
PLANS DATA
No. of sheets: 4 plus instruction booklet
Level of detail: Above average
Cost per set: $60.00
WB Plan No. 86

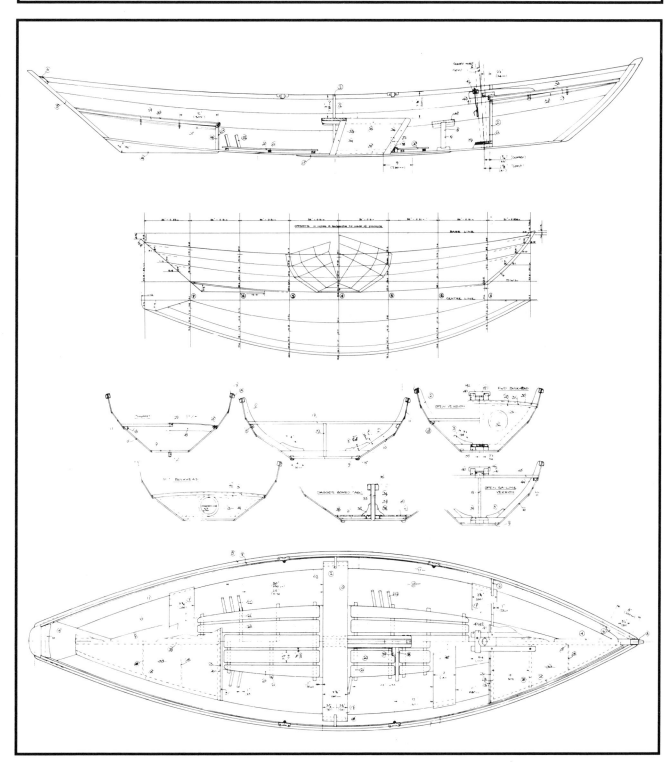

18'3" John Dory

by Iain Oughtred

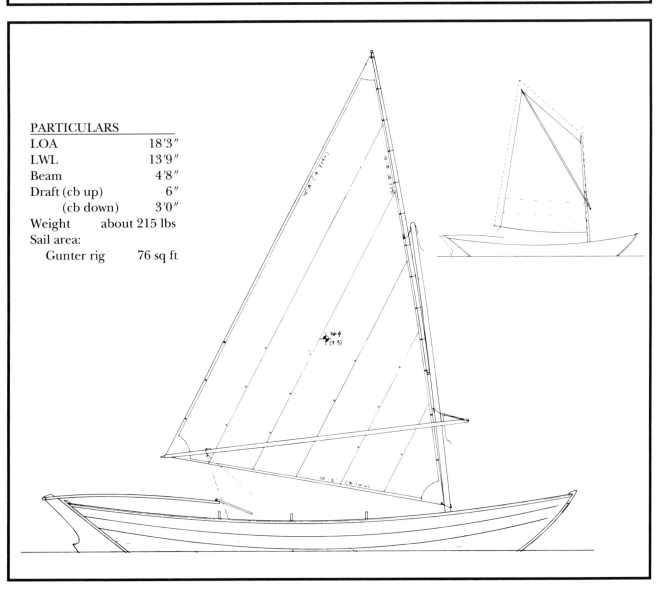

PARTICULARS

LOA	18'3"
LWL	13'9"
Beam	4'8"
Draft (cb up)	6"
(cb down)	3'0"
Weight	about 215 lbs
Sail area:	
Gunter rig	76 sq ft

Development of the Swampscott dory as a pleasure boat reaches back almost 100 years, marking this type as one of the earliest traditional small sailing craft to be converted from commercial to recreational use.

Iain Oughtred's interpretation of a Swampscott comes as a fresh and welcome addition to what is, by this time, a crowded field of published dory designs. His John Dory is distinguished not only by its fine appearance, but by the wealth of technical information contained in this single set of plans.

For example, Oughtred has provided no fewer than nine alternative sail rigs for this boat. The boat itself abounds with options—buoyancy compartments, motor-well, workboat specs—making this many vessels in one, and allowing the builder an unusual range of choices.

The John Dory can be built conventionally with solid lumber. But Oughtred favors the use of glued-seam lap-strake plywood over sawn frames; by way of encourage-

ment and assistance, he has supplied a step-by-step in-struction booklet, illustrating the building procedure.

No lofting is required; full-sized patterns are supplied for frames, stem, and transom. Oughtred has also worked up a detailed fastenings schedule and a materials list, both of which reduce time spent in making calculations and encourage accurate, economical shopping for this boat.

When she's done, the John Dory makes a light, lively sailer that is also a true pleasure to row; her hull form is exceptionally seaworthy. She's a handsome, round-sided boat with a narrow, flat bottom that makes her beachable and keeps her upright, once out of the water.

Plans are on six sheets and include lines, basic rig, construction plan and setup, full-sized patterns, and op-tional sail plans. Construction notes, materials list, and the 13-page illustrated monograph on building proce-dures accompany the set. WB Plan No. 81. $75.00.

Plan 81

DESCRIPTION

Hull type: Flat-bottomed, round-sided dory
Rig: Optional; 9 sail plans (55 sq ft to 94 sq ft)
Construction: Glued lapstrake plywood over sawn
  frames

PERFORMANCE

*Suitable for: Protected waters
*Intended capacity: 2–4
  Trailerable: Yes

See page 78 for further information.

Propulsion: Sail, oars, outboard
Speed (knots): 2–4

BUILDING DATA

Skill needed: Basic to intermediate
Lofting required: No
*Alternative construction: Traditional dory
  construction

PLANS DATA

No. of sheets: 5 plus instruction booklet
Level of detail: Above average
Cost per set: $75.00
WB Plan No. 81

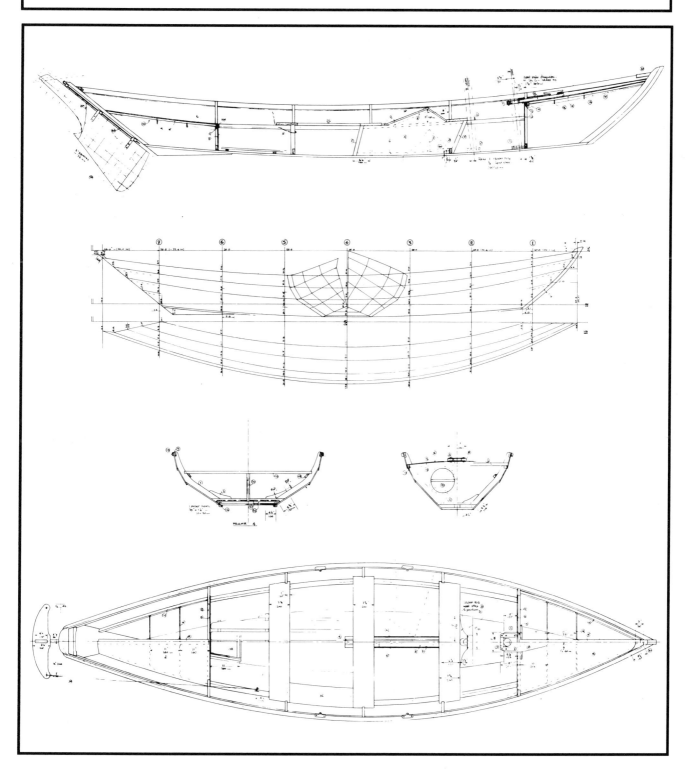

14′ Catamaran, Pixie

by Richard and Lilian Woods

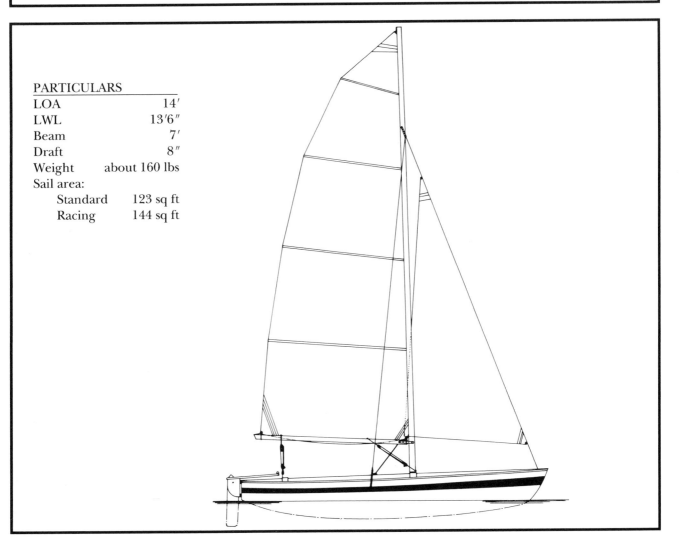

PARTICULARS	
LOA	14′
LWL	13′6″
Beam	7′
Draft	8″
Weight	about 160 lbs
Sail area:	
Standard	123 sq ft
Racing	144 sq ft

Pixie is the first multihull to be offered in *WoodenBoat*'s catalog of plans. This sloop was selected for design elements that separate her from other contemporary catamarans and that overcome certain objections to multihulls in general.

Pixie is, we feel, easy to build. Construction is by the stitch-and-glue method, using sheet plywood over bulkhead frames, which makes fast work of a small-boat building project such as this one. No lofting is required. Richard and Lilian Woods—multihull specialists from Cornwall, England, who designed Pixie—estimate a total of about 80 hours of orderly but by no means intensive labor to construct and complete this boat.

Another reason for ease of construction is found in the plans themselves, which are not merely mechanical drawings, but a fully rendered guide to the building and rigging of this boat, with detailed specifications for materials and fittings. The plans are so clear as to resemble drawings for a how-to magazine article, or assembly instructions for a kit boat-in-a-box; they are a great visual aid for a vessel that is, in fact, being made by hand.

The completed craft is light, and, what's more, can be dismantled using a special slot-together system that requires no wrenches or keys. The whole works can thus be cartopped: there's no need to worry about trailering, or storing, a wide and awkward load. Each hull weighs about 40 lbs; and the entire outfit weighs about 160 lbs.

The V-bottomed form of each hull gives this 14-footer a good bite in the water without need of dagger- or centerboards, and minimizes as well the possibility of pitchpoling. Tilt-up rudders enable this cat to be sailed onto and off a beach.

Pixie is fast—high-performance fast—without being over-canvased and too hot to handle in a stiff breeze. This is a safe boat for a crew of one or two, and features a standard sloop rig with a fully battened main. A second or racing sail plan of increased area is also included.

Pixie's plans are on three large sheets which contain the building data, dimensions, rigging specifications, and illustrations for her construction sequence and fitting out. A separate, smaller sheet itemizes requisite materials and fastenings. WB Plan No. 83. $75.00.

Plan 83

DESCRIPTION
Hull type: V-bottomed catamaran
Rig: Sloop
Construction: Stitch-and-glue plywood over
    bulkhead frames
PERFORMANCE
*Suitable for: Protected waters
*Intended capacity: 1–2

See page 78 for further information.

Trailerable: Cartop
Propulsion: Sail
Speed (knots): 12–15
BUILDING DATA
Skill needed: Basic
Lofting required: No
*Alternative construction: None
PLANS DATA
No. of sheets: 3
Level of detail: Above average
Cost per set: $75.00
WB Plan No. 83

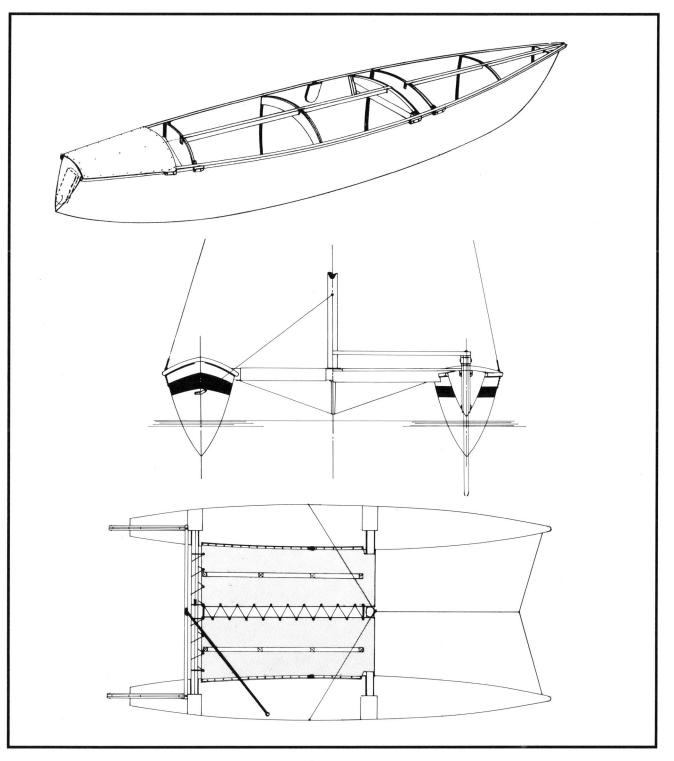

14′5″ Biscayne Bay Sailing Skiff

by Nathanael G. Herreshoff

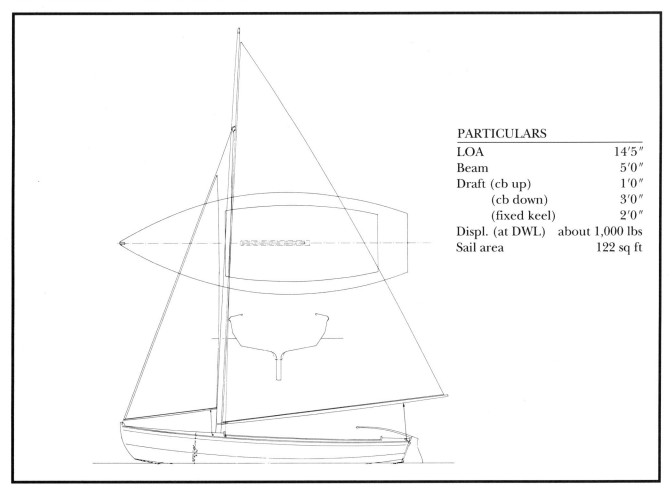

PARTICULARS	
LOA	14′5″
Beam	5′0″
Draft (cb up)	1′0″
(cb down)	3′0″
(fixed keel)	2′0″
Displ. (at DWL)	about 1,000 lbs
Sail area	122 sq ft

Whether designed as an AMERICA's Cup defender or the tender for it, each of N.G. Herreshoff's yachts was very carefully thought through, and then critically examined. The comparatively simple skiff presented here is no exception. After studying the fleet of these for their first season, Herreshoff commented, "They have proved a great success, being safe, fast, and able, and they handle beautifully." A dozen of these skiffs were built in 1925 for the Adirondack School, which had a station at Coconut Grove.

Originally intended for the shoal Florida waters for which the design is named, this 14-footer is offered in two versions: a shallow-draft, keel-and-centerboard combination, or a deep-draft fixed iron keel. The second version is the easier of the two to build, and better to windward, but the original model will float in a mere foot of water, and, of course, be handier to trailer. In addition to the keel options there are some interesting construction features that put this boat a cut above anything like it—but still within reach of the skills of an amateur builder.

The Herreshoffs were noted for strong construction using light scantlings. The Biscayne Bay boat has a double-chined hull planked with solid wood and timbered with steam-bent half-frames (that is, the frames

stop short of the keel where they connect with floor timbers). This knuckled hull looks better than a single-chined, V-bottomed hull of plywood construction, and behaves more like a round-bottomed boat when heeled.

Beneath the foredeck is a watertight compartment: side decks and cockpit sole accommodate the crew. So there are no seats or hatches to build, and the boat has reserve buoyancy in the unlikely event of a capsize. The rudder profile is unusual, but its construction is not—this shape increases directional stability without exceeding the boat's minimum draft.

Because the Herreshoffs preferred to custom cast much of the hardware for their yachts, drawings are supplied for this boat's original fittings—if the builder is so inclined to make or obtain castings. Alternatively, stock hardware can be substituted, as indicated in the plans.

This sailing skiff will make a fine building project and an excellent day boat when done. She has the added distinction of having been designed by the best. Six sheets of plans, two of which were developed as supplements by WoodenBoat, show construction and offsets, keel and rudder details, spar details, sail plan, sails, rigging, fittings, ballast keel, stem details, hull sections, and boom crotch. WB Plan No. 66. $75.00.

Plan 66

DESCRIPTION
Hull type: V-bottomed, double-chined daysailer
Rig: Marconi sloop
Construction: Batten-seam planking over steamed frames

PERFORMANCE
*Suitable for: Protected waters
*Intended capacity: 2–4

*See page 78 for further information.

Trailerable: Yes
Propulsion: Sail or sculling oar
Speed (knots): 2–4
BUILDING DATA
Skill needed: Intermediate
Lofting required: Optional
*Alternative construction: Plywood
PLANS DATA
No. of sheets: 6
Level of detail: Above average
Cost per set: $75.00
WB Plan No. 66

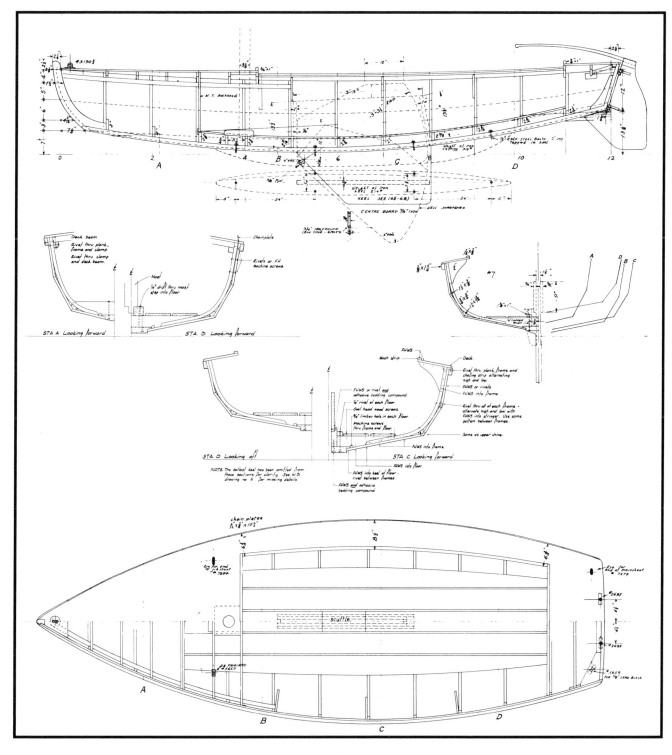

16′ Haven 12¹/₂ Class

by Joel White

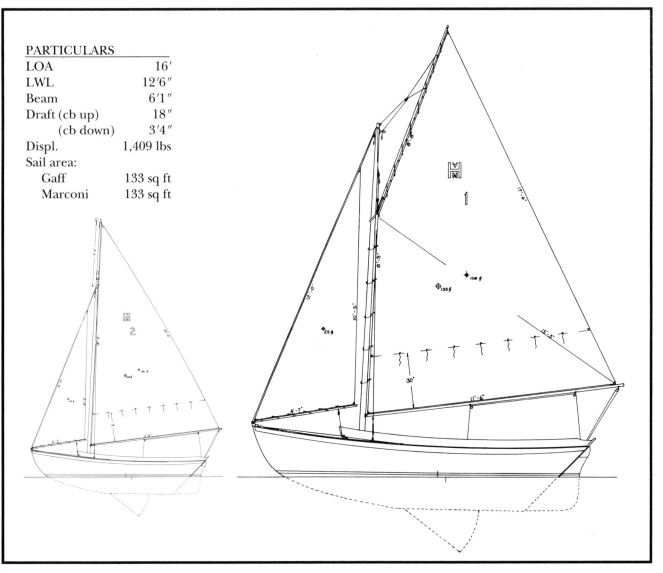

PARTICULARS

LOA	16′
LWL	12′6″
Beam	6′1″
Draft (cb up)	18″
(cb down)	3′4″
Displ.	1,409 lbs
Sail area:	
Gaff	133 sq ft
Marconi	133 sq ft

The Haven 12¹/₂-footer was inspired by the history and tradition of Nathanael G. Herreshoff's renowned Herreshoff 12¹/₂, a class of keelboats just under 16′ long (with a waterline length of 12¹/₂′—hence the name). Long known for their seaworthiness, their charm, and their fine turn of speed, the Herreshoff 12¹/₂'s, or Bullseyes, as the marconi-rigged versions came to be known, have carried sailors young and old since 1914.

The Haven, we think, is the Herreshoff 12¹/₂ made handier, since the only alteration has been to convert the original carvel-planked, full-keeled version to a shoal-draft keel/centerboarder, giving her a slight increase in beam so as to retain the same stability. These modifications have improved her versatility while preserving performance.

The original boats were restricted to water depths of 2¹/₂′ or more, but the Haven class—which draws a full foot less water—can be sailed in shallower water, beached, and easily trailered.

Naval architect Joel White, whose Brooklin (Maine) Boat Yard maintains a number of original 12¹/₂'s, accomplished the design changeover. Maynard Bray—an expert on Herreshoff construction processes—built the first Haven to White's plans using the Herreshoff Manufacturing Company's construction methods. (Boats are built upside-down, with a station mold placed at every frame location, such that each frame is bent over a mold.) The construction sequence was carefully documented, and we are pleased to publish the results of the White/Bray collaboration on this loveliest of daysailers.

The manual *How to Build the Haven 12¹/₂-Footer* by Maynard Bray, with step-by-step photographs by Anne Bray and illustrations by Kathy Bray, is $15.00. Building plans by Joel White consist of eight sheets which include lines, construction, two sail plans (gaff and marconi), spars, hardware, and bulkhead details. Full-sized mold patterns are also provided, eliminating the need for lofting. Price for the plans set only is $180.00. WB Plan No. 75.

Plan 75

DESCRIPTION
Hull type: Round-bottomed, keel/centerboard
Rig: Gaff or marconi sloop
Construction: Carvel planked over steam-bent
    frames

PERFORMANCE
*Suitable for: Somewhat protected waters
*Intended capacity: 3–6 daysailing
  Trailerable: Yes

See page 78 for further information.

Propulsion: Sail
Speed (knots): 3–5

BUILDING DATA
Skill needed: Advanced
Lofting required: No
*Alternative construction: None
Helpful information: *How to Build the Haven 12½-
    Footer,* by Maynard Bray

PLANS DATA
No. of sheets: 8
Level of detail: Above average
Cost per set: $180.00
WB Plan No. 75

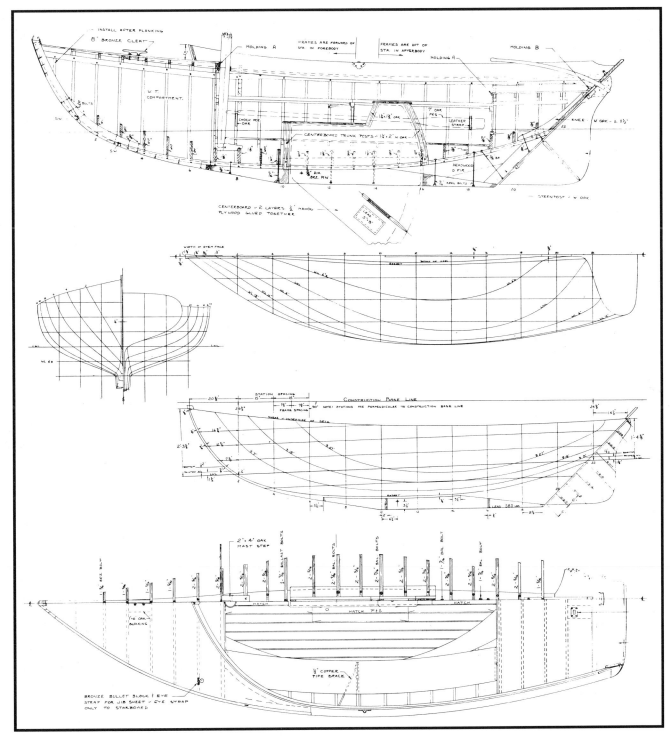

18'6" Canoe Yawl, Eel

by William Garden

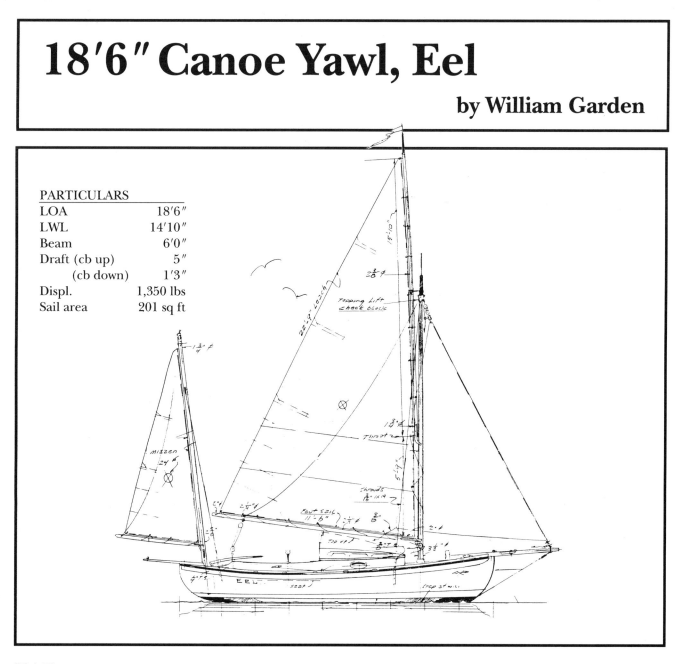

PARTICULARS

LOA	18'6"
LWL	14'10"
Beam	6'0"
Draft (cb up)	5"
(cb down)	1'3"
Displ.	1,350 lbs
Sail area	201 sq ft

We've long admired Bill Garden's canoe yawl Eel, and we're pleased that he has redrawn her plans for WoodenBoat. This delightful little design is named for a 19th-century British cruiser drawn by George Holmes. The original Eel was larger and heavier than our Eel, but the two boats have a family resemblance in the double-ended hull form and the yawl rig.

While our Eel follows the original canoe yawl theme, the construction has been arranged to incorporate today's materials for building by either strip or cold-molded methods.

In form she is similar to a large sailing dinghy. She has no reverse curves in her sections and is of light displacement, making trailering and beaching easy. For a boat that is to be put ashore regularly, the lead outside ballast can be omitted and a similar amount of shot bags carried inside and put ashore prior to hauling her up on the beach.

The simple yawl rig requires a minimum of purchased fittings. The mast is short, but sufficient sail area has been achieved by fitting an efficient gunter rig. Spars stow on board for trailering, and the bowsprit and boomkin can be arranged to unbolt and shorten her up for storage.

For spartan overnight cruising a small cuddy cabin is shown with hinged top to allow better sitting headroom below. She can be built with this cabin or simply as an open dayboat with a large party cockpit. Some Eels have been built with folding canvas shelter cabins.

The shoal-draft centerboard arrangement opens up usually inaccessible shallow bays and estuaries that often prove to be the most interesting coastal cruising spots. For very shallow waters or for beaching, the rudder can be retracted vertically, and she can then be steered with an oar out either quarter. Stand-up raised oarlocks are shown to help her along in a calm. A small outboard (about 4 hp) clamped on a bracket will move her along at about 4½ knots.

Four sheets of plans are provided, showing sail and spar details, arrangement, and lines and offsets. Construction details include sections for carvel, cold-molded, or strip planking. WB Plan No. 90. $100.00.

Plan 90

DESCRIPTION
Hull type: Round-bottomed canoe yawl
Rig: Yawl
Construction: Strip, cold-molded, or carvel
Headroom/cabin: About 3′
PERFORMANCE
*Suitable for: Somewhat protected waters
*Intended capacity: 3–6 daysailing

*See page 78 for further information.

Trailerable: Yes
Propulsion: Sail, oar, outboard
Speed (knots): 3–5
BUILDING DATA
Skill needed: Intermediate to advanced
Lofting required: Yes
*Alternative construction: Lapstrake
PLANS DATA
No. of sheets: 4
Level of detail: Average
Cost per set: $100.00
WB Plan No. 90

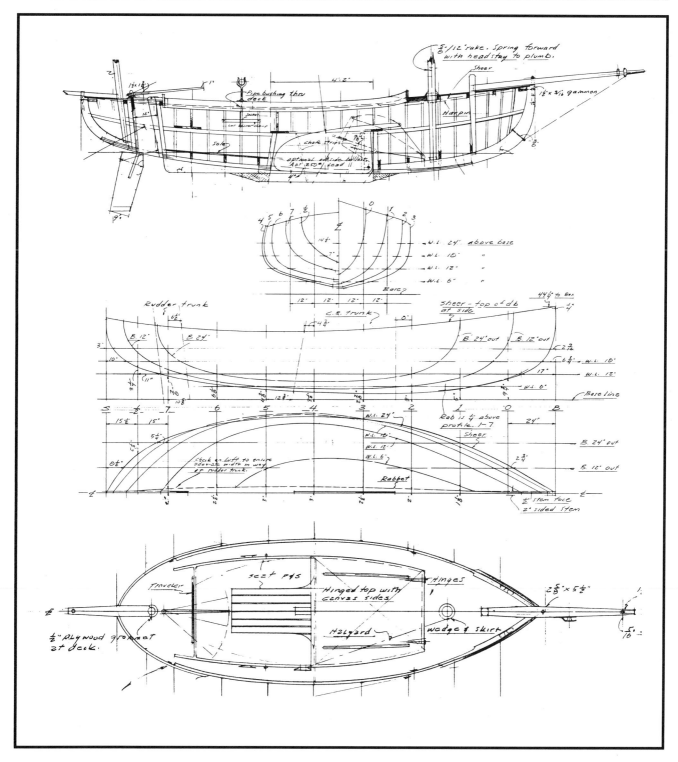

19'6" Centerboard Sloop, Triton

by Robert M. Steward

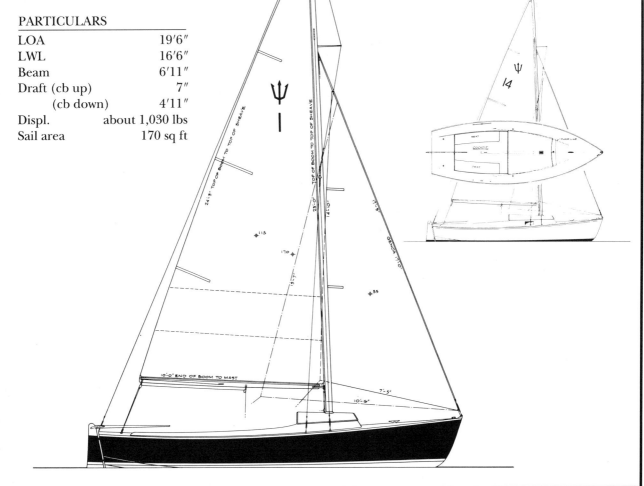

PARTICULARS

LOA	19'6"
LWL	16'6"
Beam	6'11"
Draft (cb up)	7"
(cb down)	4'11"
Displ.	about 1,030 lbs
Sail area	170 sq ft

True, this boat does not have a clipper bow, gaff rig, and elliptical transom. But she can be constructed without difficulty, sailed smartly, and her credentials are among the best.

Triton was designed by Bob Steward, who literally wrote the book on small-craft construction—*Boatbuilding Manual,* now in its third edition. That book began with this boat, when *The Rudder* magazine, shortly after World War II, commissioned Steward to design "a safe, wholesome daysailer with a moderate sail plan." He followed this design with a series of boatbuilding articles that were later compiled into a book that was then expanded into the present manual. In a real sense, it can be regarded as the companion volume for the construction of this sailboat.

He gave Triton an arc-bottomed hull, making it comparatively simple to loft (all bottom sections between the chine and centerline are arcs of the same circle) and to build. She is best built upside down, and can be either carvel-planked or ship-lapped—or even double-planked, if desired.

The sail plan, with less than 200 sq ft, is substantially stayed—which suggests a fast boat. Indeed, *The Rudder* also sought a one-design class racer in Triton. Add to that her cuddy—available in long or short versions— and you have a small, simple racer, cruiser that looks as good and competitive as many production boats presently on the market. Her centerboard is fabricated of galvanized steel, kept low in the cockpit but shaped for maximum lateral stability when down. The hull draws only 7" with the board up.

Triton has generous beam and freeboard, making her stable and dry. She is readily trailerable for her size (though the rig is not readily struck), and would be a handy boat at the lake or shore. She would in addition be easy to store (she'll fit in a normal-sized garage) and maintain. There is much to recommend this boat as a family daysailer and bare-minimum overnighter.

Seven sheets of plans include outboard profile, sail plan, lines and offsets, construction, spar details, rigging tangs, and construction plan for the lengthened cuddy. WB Plan 67. $90.00.

Plan 67

DESCRIPTION
Hull type: Arc-bottomed centerboard boat
Rig: Marconi sloop
Construction: Carvel planked over sawn frames
Headroom/cabin (between beams): About 3′1″
PERFORMANCE
*Suitable for: Somewhat protected waters
*Intended capacity: 2–4 daysailing, 2 cruising

*See page 78 for further information.

Trailerable: Yes
Propulsion: Sail
Speed (knots): 3–5
BUILDING DATA
Skill needed: Intermediate
Lofting required: Yes
*Alternative construction: Strip, or strip bottom with plywood sides
PLANS DATA
No. of sheets: 7
Level of detail: Above average
Cost per set: $90.00
WB Plan No. 67

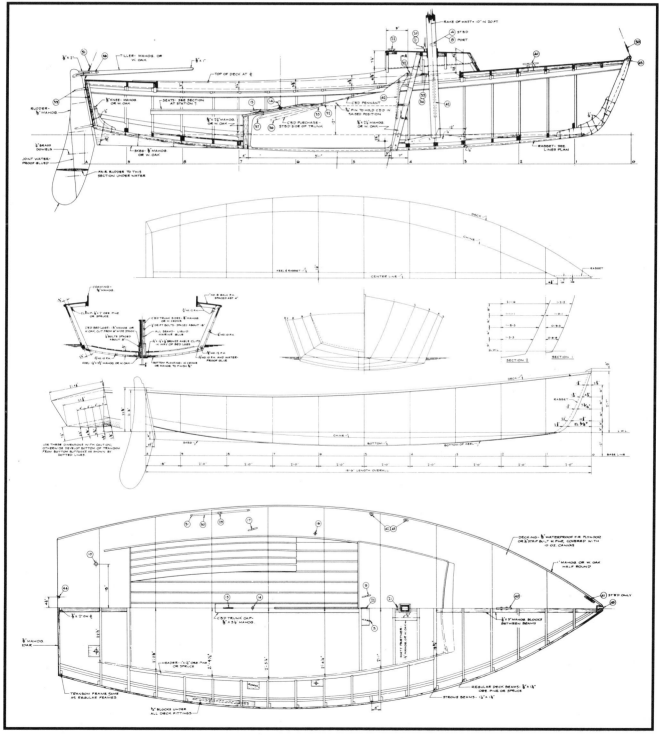

19'9" Drascombe Peter Boat

by John Watkinson

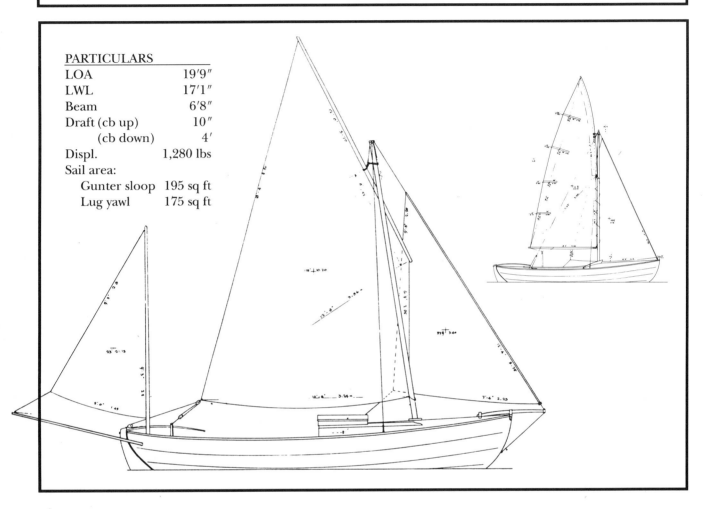

PARTICULARS

LOA	19'9"
LWL	17'1"
Beam	6'8"
Draft (cb up)	10"
(cb down)	4'
Displ.	1,280 lbs
Sail area:	
Gunter sloop	195 sq ft
Lug yawl	175 sq ft

A quarter-century has passed since British designer John Watkinson introduced the Lugger, his first Drascombe—an 18'6" gunter yawl, versions of which soon logged several remarkable open-boat voyages (one of these was a singlehanded passage from England to Australia in 1969–70). The long-distance achievements of these craft over the years have proven their cruising abilities and generated a demand for Drascombes in a variety of different sizes and configurations.

The Peter Boat presented here is the latest addition to an expanding fleet. At 19'9" she is a bit larger than the original Lugger, and incorporates various elements drawn from the full line of Drascombe designs. She is the first Drascombe model to be made generally available as a set of plans, for which WoodenBoat arranged to combine Watkinson's design work with Iain Oughtred's detailing and draftsmanship. The result is a complete folio of drawings directed at the skilled amateur builder.

This vessel is evocative of the inshore working craft of Britain. But she is not a replica sailboat or a derivative modified for modern construction. The design is thoroughly original and shaped for glued-seam lapstrake plywood planking over sawn frames and bulkheads—a building system Watkinson helped develop. His Peter Boat has the rounded, knuckled sides and wide strakes of our North Shore dories; she is a double-ender with a North Sea stern and a moderate V-bottom.

Bulkheads and sawn framing add further stiffness to a tough hull. Steel plate is specified for both the centerboard and the pivoted rudder blade, thus adding material strength to chronically vulnerable parts, while enabling the boat to be easily beached or trailered. An outboard motorwell is a discreet and integral feature in this as in all the Drascombes.

Both sail and interior arrangements are flexible, which broadens both the possibilities and the appeal of this practical and attractive design. The Peter Boat can be built as a daysailer, with or without decking; or as a camper-cruiser, with a short cuddy or a long cabin, and alternative cockpit layouts. She can be set up as a gunter sloop, with a gracefully curved "bird's-wing" yard and an all-inboard rig; or as a standing-lug yawl, with a demountable bowsprit and boomkin. All options are fully detailed.

Five sheets of plans contain this Drascombe's lines, construction plan and details, two sail plans, and optional layouts. Three pages of specifications are included. WB Plan No. 82. $90.00.

Plan 82

DESCRIPTION
Hull type: V-bottomed centerboarder
Rig: Gunter sloop or lug yawl
Construction: Glued lapstrake plywood over plywood frames and bulkheads
Headroom/cabin (between beams): About 2′6″
PERFORMANCE
*Suitable for: Somewhat protected waters
*Intended capacity: 3–6 daysailing, 2 cruising
*See page 78 for further information.

Trailerable: Yes
Propulsion: Sail, outboard
Speed (knots): 3–5
BUILDING DATA
Skill needed: Intermediate to advanced
Lofting required: Yes
*Alternative construction: None
PLANS DATA
No. of sheets: 5
Level of detail: Average
Cost per set: $90.00
WB Plan No. 82

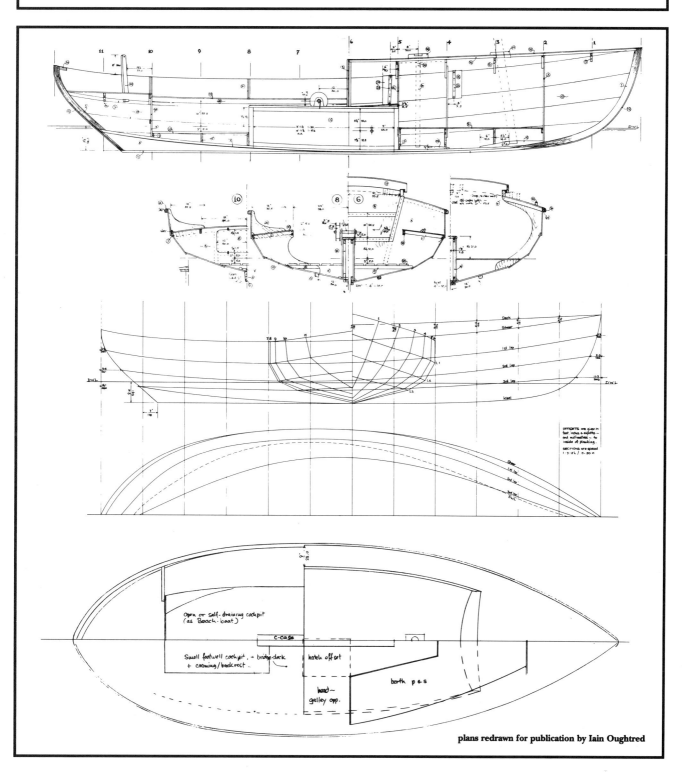

Open or self-draining cockpit (as Beach-boat)

C-case

Small footwell cockpit, + bridge-deck + coaming/backrest

hatch offset

head — galley opp.

berth p & s

plans redrawn for publication by Iain Oughtred

—33—

14'6" Outboard Skiff, Little Moby

by Charles Wittholz

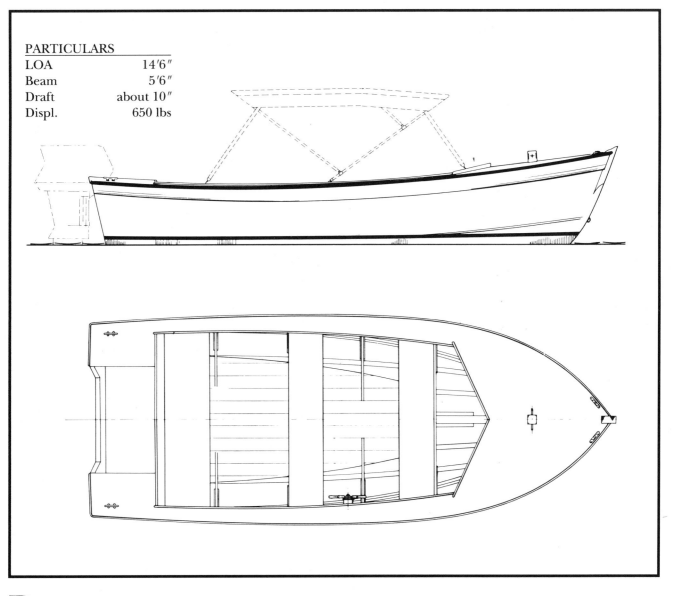

PARTICULARS

LOA	14'6"
Beam	5'6"
Draft	about 10"
Displ.	650 lbs

Designer Charles Wittholz describes his Little Moby as a rough-water skiff. She is surely that, but she is also an excellent craft for slow cruising alongshore or fishing on an inland lake. Her V-bottom has deep deadrise for easy motion in disturbed seas and a flat run aft for good performance under moderate outboard power. High freeboard makes her a dry boat with substantial reserve stability.

This hull design is similar to, though smaller than, Wittholz's 18' outboard runabout — Downeaster (WB Plan No. 71)—whose construction was covered in several issues of *WoodenBoat* magazine (WB Nos. 73, 74, and 75). Those articles produced a number of requests for a smaller version of that boat in the 12–16' range. Little Moby is the fine-looking result.

Like her big sister, she's a good project for the builder with average woodworking skills. She's constructed of ply-wood over sawn frames; an optional wale strake of ply or hard wood adds strength and character to the sheer.

Among the features on this boat are: side-mounted wheel-steering (an uncommon but practical arrange-ment); provision for a demountable "Bimini" canvas top (for weather protection); and a bona fide, deck-to-keel mooring bitt (for anchoring and mooring security).

Though only a 14½-footer, Little Moby can comforta-bly accommodate five people, and is rated for outboard engines up to 40 hp. An interesting "combination" craft, she's laid out like a classic launch, with decking and steering details—and built like a sea skiff, able to take it.

This Wittholz outboard can be constructed without lofting, thanks to a detailed framing setup plan, one of the five sheets in the set—which also includes lines, off-sets, construction, general arrangement, profile, and deck plan. WB Plan No. 77. $60.00.

Plan 77

DESCRIPTION
Hull type: V-bottomed
Construction: Plywood planking over sawn frames
PERFORMANCE
*Suitable for: Somewhat protected waters
*Intended capacity: 2–6, day cruising
Trailerable: Yes

See page 78 for further information.

Propulsion: 10–40-hp outboard
Speed: 20–30 mph
BUILDING DATA
Skill needed: Basic to intermediate
Lofting required: No
*Alternative construction: None
PLANS DATA
No. of sheets: 5
Level of detail: Above average
Cost per set: $60.00
WB Plan No. 77

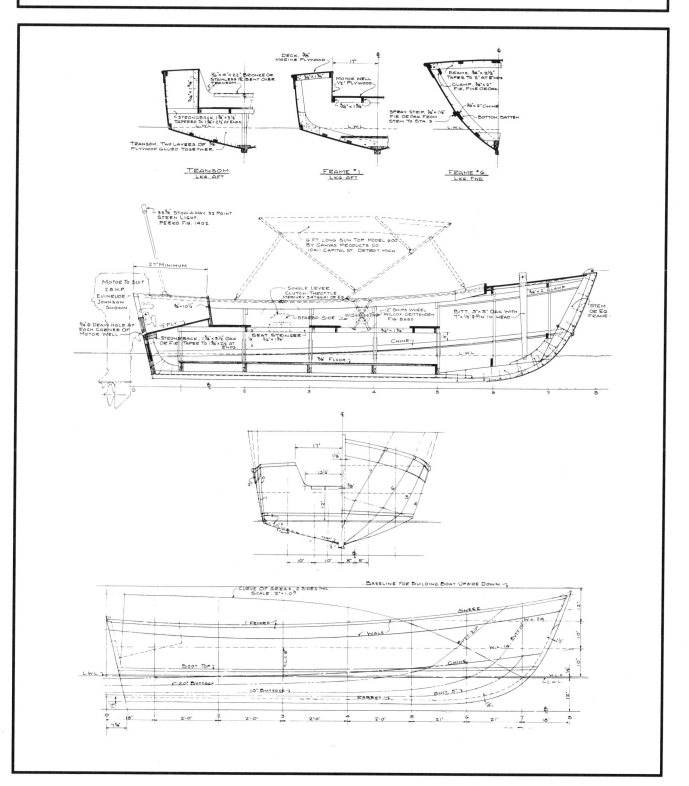

16′ Gentleman's Runabout

by Nelson Zimmer and John Hacker

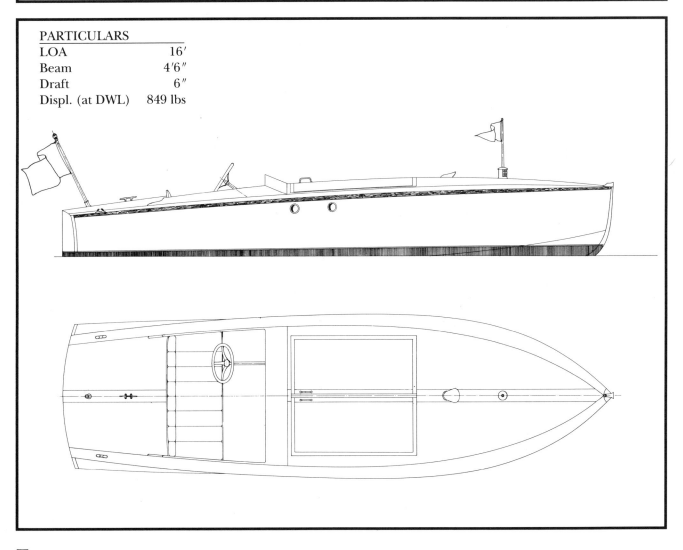

PARTICULARS

LOA	16′
Beam	4′6″
Draft	6″
Displ. (at DWL)	849 lbs

Inboard-powered mahogany runabouts are on the water again, and on the increase, after near-extinction in a fiberglass marketplace. Even so, given the new wave of restorations and reproductions, this 16-footer by Zimmer and Hacker remains unique.

John Hacker was one of this country's great names in the design and development of pleasure and racing powerboats. Nelson Zimmer, who was informally associated with Hacker after World War II, has to date designed three other small craft for *WoodenBoat*'s catalog of plans.

The runabout presented here is according to Zimmer, "based on the creative genius of the late John L. Hacker." She is not an easy boat to build; but then, no runabout worthy of the name ever was, which is why these boats continue to spark interest and hold value.

Her construction is conventional for a craft of this type: batten-seam mahogany planking over sawn frames. This is a method that holds up well over time and keeps a dry-sailed boat dry in the water, without the need to wait for swelling to close up her seams.

This is a runabout by an earlier, more elegant, defini-tion of the term: a pleasure boat for gentle men and women. The Zimmer–Hacker craft can take two people out not just for a spin, but for an experience. Powerboating may have become faster than this, but not better. She can do 30 mph—max; thus, she is more like a two-seat country roadster of the period than a pounding offshore racer of the present. Strict limitations have been placed on the power plant—so that the hull strength will not be exceeded.

Nelson Zimmer is noted for his attention to detail; in that regard, this homage to Hacker is Zimmer at his best. For example, as a clear aid to construction, he has drawn sections of each of the building-frame stations; and in the interest of authenticity, he has provided measured drawings for the boat's custom hardware and fittings.

Here, then, is a little beauty deserving of the phrase "for the discerning yachtsman." And, we might add, "for the discriminating craftsman."

Five sheets of plans include profile and deck arrange-ment, lines and offsets, construction plan, construction sections, and assorted fittings. WB Plan No. 76. $120.00.

Plan 76

DESCRIPTION
Hull type: V-bottomed runabout
Construction: Battened-seam planking over sawn frames

PERFORMANCE
*Suitable for: Protected waters
*Intended capacity: 1–2
Trailerable: Yes

See page 78 for further information.

Propulsion: Gas inboard engine
Speed: 30 mph

BUILDING DATA
Skill needed: Advanced
Lofting required: Yes
*Alternative construction: None

PLANS DATA
No. of sheets: 5
Level of detail: Average
Cost per set: $120.00
WB Plan No. 76

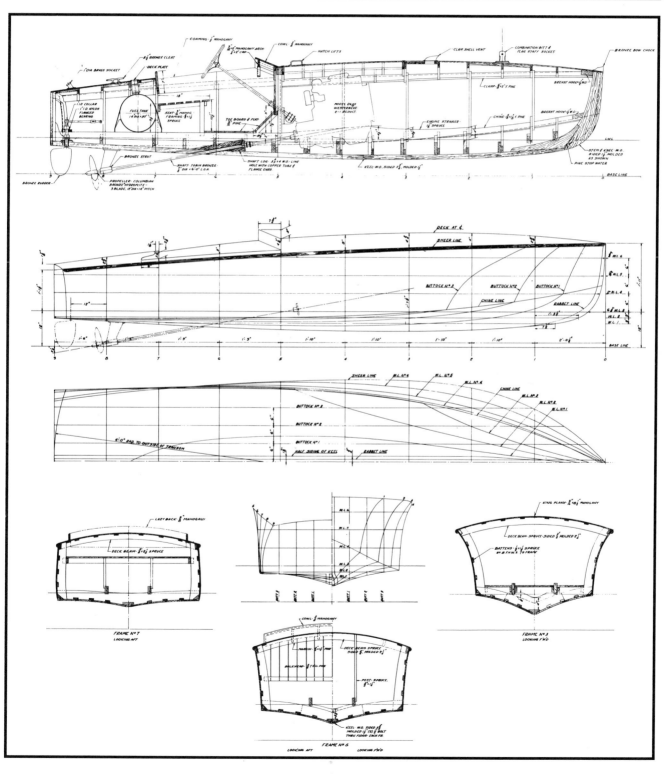

18' Plywood Runabout, Downeaster

by Charles Wittholz

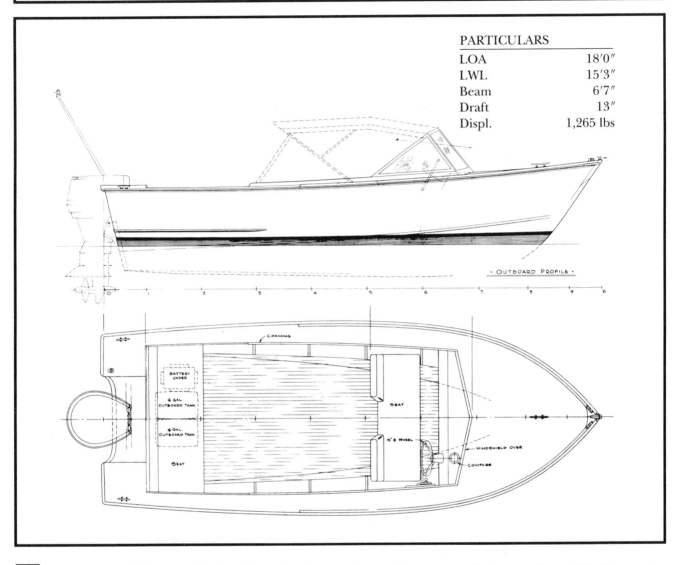

PARTICULARS

LOA	18'0"
LWL	15'3"
Beam	6'7"
Draft	13"
Displ.	1,265 lbs

· OUTBOARD PROFILE ·

The Downeaster 18 is arguably the all-American boat in this catalog of boat plans, the kind of craft one sees on any major body of water here—fresh or salty—or on the road heading for it. However, at least three features distinguish Downeaster from most production powerboats in the 18' range, currently in circulation.

First, we think she is much better looking. Second, she is certainly more versatile—as a hull for all waters, especially choppy ones; and in the two arrangements available (a runabout with split windshield and convertible top, or a center-console fisherman with canvas dodger).

Third, she can be built at home using standard plywood construction over sawn frames, and requiring no steam bending or complex carpentry. Moreover, *WoodenBoat* documented the building of a Downeaster in three successive issues of the magazine (WB Nos. 73, 74, and 75)—amounting to a virtual how-to-build workbook for this boat.

In the standard outboard runabout version, Downeaster also features full-width seats forward and aft (with

plenty of open space in between), a self-bailing motorwell, and sufficient decking forward and along the sides to help keep the interior, the crew, and the day's gear reasonably dry. Power range is 40–100 hp; a 75-hp unit can readily deliver 30 mph. The same characteristics that make the boat swift and responsive (narrow, deep-V hull) make her very suitable for waterskiing, as well. With an appropriate tow-bar setup, Downeaster will make an excellent ski boat.

The boat has satisfied these critical design criteria: handsome appearance; economy and durability of construction; and a hull form that gives good performance underway, at all speeds and in a variety of sea conditions. In addition, the Downeaster 18 is burdensome in the best sense: this boat will carry six persons—safely and comfortably.

The plans are well detailed on five sheets: lines and offsets, construction sections, a construction plan, and arrangements for both the utility runabout and center-console models. WB Plan No. 71. $90.00.

Plan 71

DESCRIPTION
Hull type: V-bottomed
Construction: Plywood planking over sawn frames
PERFORMANCE
*Suitable for: Somewhat protected waters
*Intended capacity: 2–6 day cruising
Trailerable: Yes

* See page 78 for further information.

Propulsion: 40–100 hp outboard
Speed: 26–40 mph
BUILDING DATA
Skill needed: Basic to intermediate
Lofting required: Yes
*Alternative construction: None
"How to build" instructions: WB Nos. 73, 74 & 75
PLANS DATA
No. of sheets: 5
Level of detail: Above average
Cost per set: $90.00
WB Plan No. 71

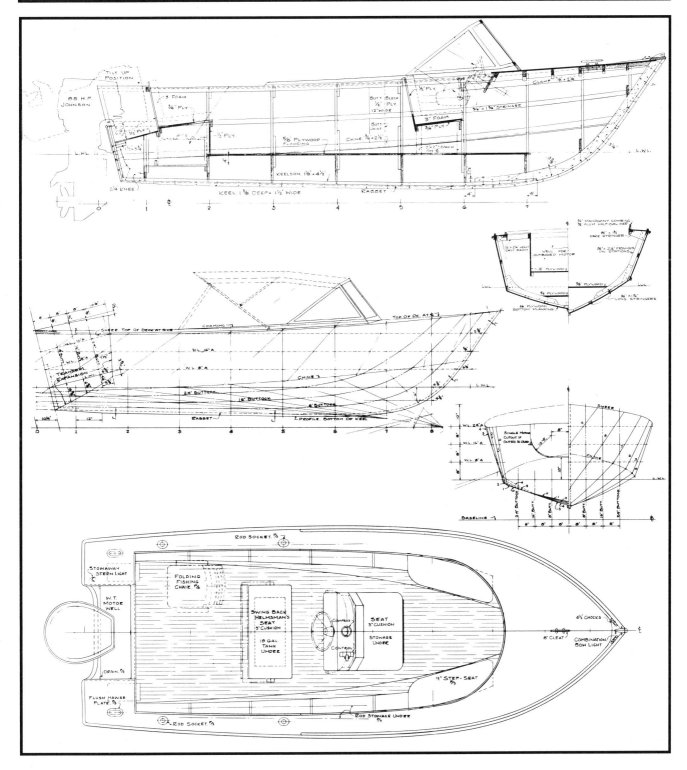

18'7" Utility Launch, Barbara Anne

by Robert M. Steward

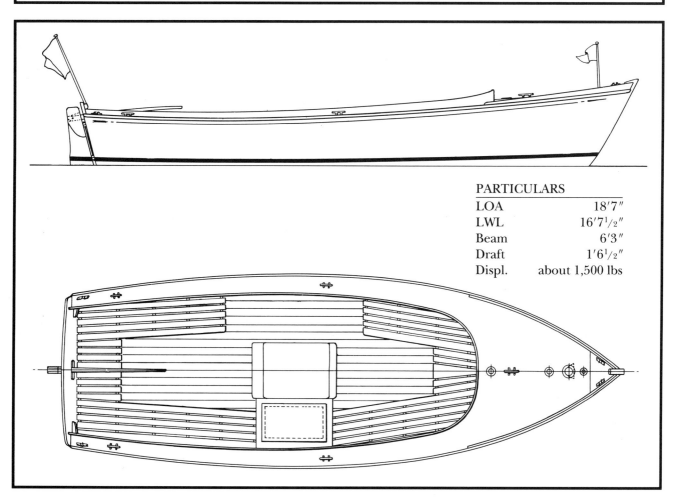

PARTICULARS	
LOA	18'7"
LWL	16'7½"
Beam	6'3"
Draft	1'6½"
Displ.	about 1,500 lbs

For as long as motors have been installed in boats, there have been people who prefer low-powered, round-bottomed hulls that deliver only a moderate turn of speed, but do so comfortably and easily. There is a growing interest in this kind of boating—powerboating as distinct from speedboating—for a variety of reasons, among them rising fuel costs.

In response to this special interest, WoodenBoat in 1984 asked naval architect Bob Steward to design the launch presented here. Barbara Anne—an outgrowth of a launch created by Steward in the early 1950s—is a lovely, all-purpose, open-cockpit, inboard-powered craft, able at sea and adaptable to all manner of waterfront activities, from ferrying to fishing to fair-weather cruising.

With a 7–10-hp diesel or similar-sized gas engine, she is economical to operate and, with her open configuration, simple to maintain. This boat can make speeds up to 10 knots—faster than a fast sailboat—and her tank holds enough fuel for a full day's run.

Construction is conventional carvel planking over steam-bent frames, giving her a tough hull, but with scantlings light enough for a builder working alone to handle with ease. The seats are slats, which hold up bet-ter in an open boat and are easier to build; side decking is laid on a shelf rather than on stub beams, another nice construction feature.

Barbara Anne is a scaled-down, state-of-the-art, semi-displacement hull suitable for work or pleasure. She's a lean launch, with a high, flaring bow to turn water aside, raking ends so as not to trip over herself, and a plain flat transom, relieved aesthetically by an outboard rudder, for simplified construction.

The overall attention to detail here is itself unusual for boats of this type. But then, the designer in this case is the author of *Boatbuilding Manual,* a book that has become the standard reference for small-craft construction in general and wooden boats in particular. Steward, more than most designers, is aware of the information requirements of both amateur and professional builders.

Though not shown on the drawings, Barbara Anne can be fitted with a canvas dodger or spray hood at little extra effort or expense. What is shown is an optional side-steering system employing a rudder blade beneath the boat. The plans for this launch are on three sheets: lines, off-sets, outboard profile and arrangement, and a construction plan with numerous detail drawings. There are sup-plementary specification pages. WB Plan No. 63. $75.00.

Plan 63

DESCRIPTION
Hull type: Round-bottomed
Construction: Carvel planked over steamed frames
PERFORMANCE
*Suitable for: Somewhat protected waters
*Intended capacity: 4–6 day cruising
Trailerable: Yes

*See page 78 for further information.

Propulsion: Inboard diesel or gas
Speed (knots): Up to 10
BUILDING DATA
Skill needed: Intermediate
Lofting required: Yes
*Alternative construction: Cold-molded, strip
PLANS DATA
No. of sheets: 3
Level of detail: Above average
Cost per set: $75.00
WB Plan No. 63

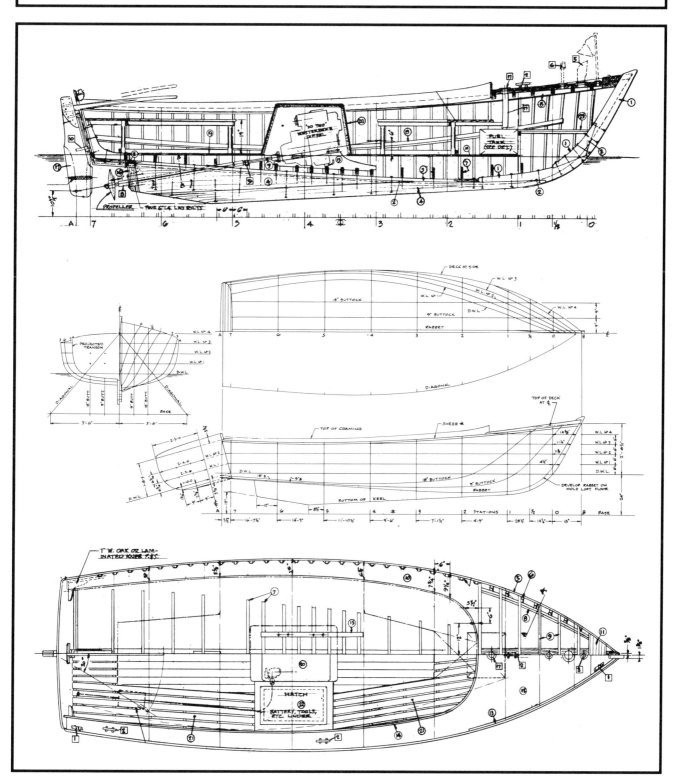

23' Fantail Launch

by Philip C. Bolger

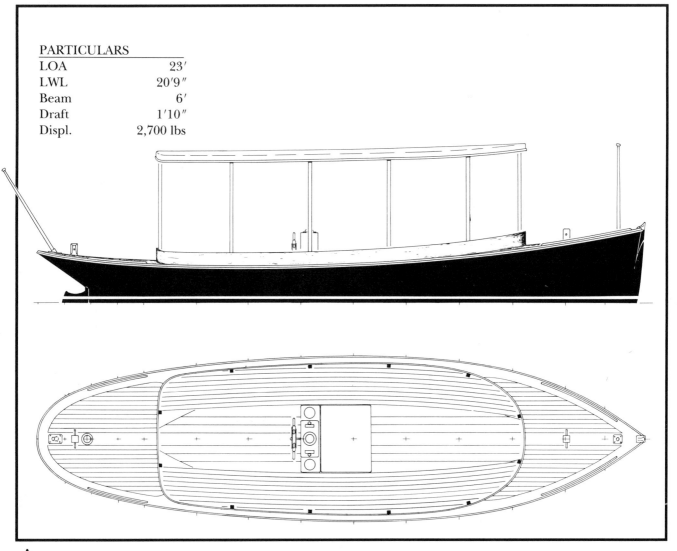

PARTICULARS

LOA	23'
LWL	20'9"
Beam	6'
Draft	1'10"
Displ.	2,700 lbs

Although we might argue that a fantail stern makes good sense because it combines substantial room on deck with an easily driven shape at the waterline, we must admit to liking this boat for purely aesthetic reasons. She's possessed of a timeless elegance that, among other things, ensures her future value.

For those familiar with Philip C. Bolger's well-publicized Instant Boats (easily built with plywood), this plan would seem to represent a radical departure for the Gloucester, Massachusetts, designer. In fact, a considerable portion of his prodigious output (more than 500 designs) displays equally shapely hulls.

This is not an easy boat to loft and set up. But builders with sufficient experience will be rewarded with a hull that presents no awkward perspectives—she'll look fine from any angle. Bolger originally intended that his launch be cold-molded: four courses to finish at $^1/_2$". However, the prototype was put together plank-on-frame by professional builder Larry Dahlmer, and our plans show both types of construction.

Bolger comments on the launch's performance: "A hull this size and shape will have a maximum possible speed of about $6^1/_4$ knots and will be happiest at about 5 knots. Probably 5 hp would be enough to produce these speeds in a dead calm and smooth sea, but she should have two or three times that power to make sure she can buck a breeze of wind and choppy water. A much larger engine will do her no harm; she might make $6^1/_2$ or even $6^3/_4$ knots, but at those speeds her forefoot will be high in the air and her stern wave will spill onto the deck. More to the point, she would become a more powerful tug."

The prototype carries sight-seers and picnickers on the Annisquam River. For that service, her designer claims she has one distinct advantage compared to contemporary powerboats—"She looks very elegant at speeds at which they look most inelegant."

Plans consist of five sheets and include lines, offsets, profile and arrangement, large-scale sections, and construction details for carvel planking and cold molding. WB Plan No. 92. $75.00.

Plan 92

DESCRIPTION
Hull type: Round-bottomed
Construction: Cold-molded or carvel-planked over
  steamed frames
PERFORMANCE
*Suitable for: Somewhat protected waters
*Intended capacity: 6–8
  Trailerable: With difficulty

See page 78 for further information.

Propulsion: 10–15-hp diesel
Speed (knots): Up to $6\frac{1}{2}$
BUILDING DATA
Skill needed: Advanced
Lofting required: Yes
*Alternative construction: Lapstrake
PLANS DATA
No. of sheets: 5
Level of detail: Average
Cost per set: $75.00
WB Plan No. 92

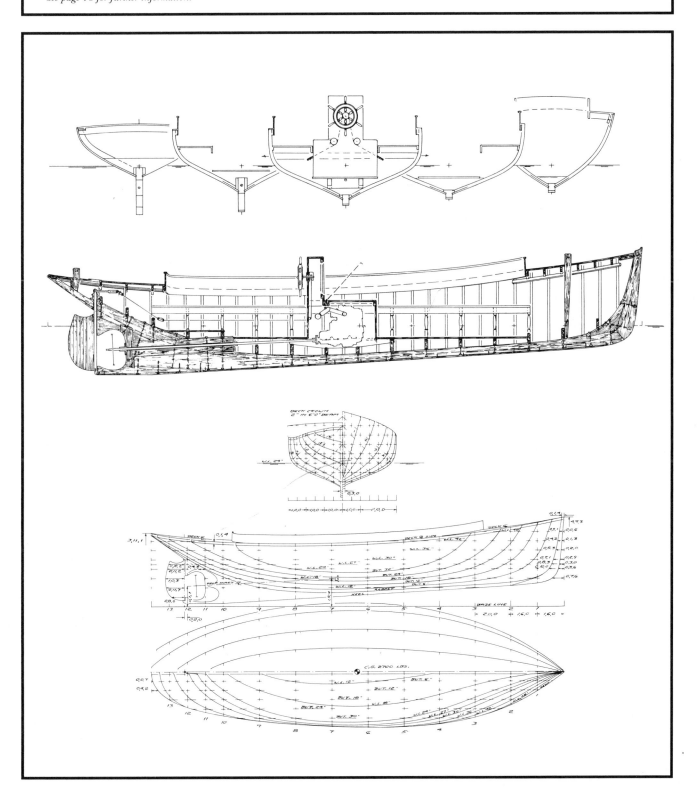

24' Angler Skiff

by Charles Wittholz

PARTICULARS

LOA	24'
LWL	21'5"
Beam	8'3½"
Draft	2'8"
Displ.	3,700 lbs

Drawn by experienced naval architect Charles Wittholz, Angler represents something of a rarity these days—a big, healthy, high-speed, open, wooden skiff with sophisticated lines. Wittholz designed this boat to provide impressive performance, and he allowed precious little compromise in hull shape. This isn't a project for neophytes.

Construction plans call for strip planking over sawn frames with a double-diagonally planked bottom. As an option, the topsides can be lapstrake plywood—a strong and light alternative whose shadow lines will accentuate Angler's shape and flare.

The lines drawings show a hull with considerable deadrise forward that flattens a little back aft in an attempt to combine the smooth high-speed ride of a deep-vee hull with sufficient stability and reasonable economy of operation. Wittholz predicts that, powered with the recommended 225–260-hp inboard engine, Angler will cruise at 24 to 30 knots and have a top speed of 24 to 36 knots.

Angler's self-bailing cockpit is deep enough to put you "in" rather than "on" the boat, and you're close to the water for easy fishing. The large space enclosed by the foredeck might serve for gear stowage or camp/cruising.

With an empty "trailer weight" of 3,700 lbs, Angler can be towed down the Interstate behind a substantial vehicle. Ready to go fishing (sportfishing, that is), the boat has an estimated weight of 4,800 lbs.

Plans for Angler are on six sheets and include profile and arrangement, lines and offsets, and three pages of construction detail. WB Plan No. 89. $150.00.

Plan 89

DESCRIPTION
Hull type: V-bottomed
Construction: Strip planking over sawn frames;
    double diagonal bottom
PERFORMANCE
*Suitable for: Somewhat protected waters
*Intended capacity: 2–8 day cruising
    Trailerable: Yes

See page 78 for further information.

Propulsion: 225–260-hp inboard
Speed (knots): 24–36
BUILDING DATA
Skill needed: Intermediate to advanced
Lofting required: Yes
*Alternative construction: Plywood lapstrake topsides
    (plans included)
PLANS DATA
No. of sheets: 6
Level of detail: Above average
Cost per set: $150.00
WB Plan No. 89

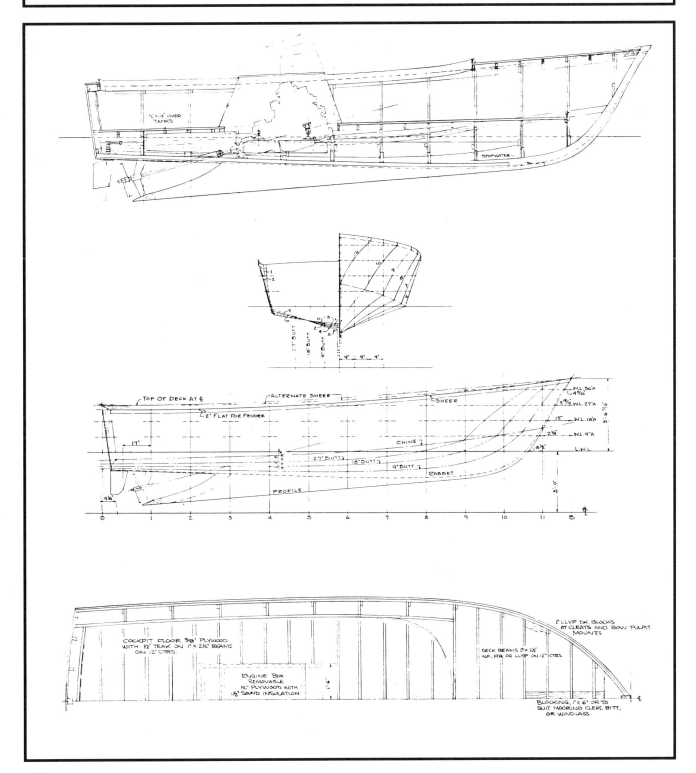

20' Sloop/Yawl, Sallee Rover

by Samuel S. Crocker

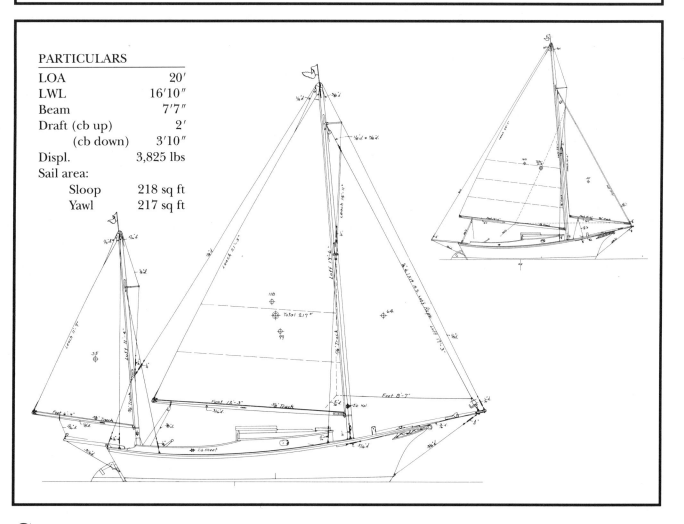

PARTICULARS

LOA	20'
LWL	16'10"
Beam	7'7"
Draft (cb up)	2'
(cb down)	3'10"
Displ.	3,825 lbs
Sail area:	
Sloop	218 sq ft
Yawl	217 sq ft

Sam Crocker's design work was highly regarded by his peers, and by those who built, brokered, maintained, or cruised his yachts. The yawl Sallee Rover, drawn in 1953, shows why this is so.

Crocker has recombined a remarkable assemblage of elements here into one small boat, but the result is so superbly proportioned that no one item overpowers the overall design. Joel White, who built the sloop version of this boat, aptly describes the hull, with its shallow draft and broad beam, as a cross between a catboat and a Muscongus Bay sloop. She has a very strong sheer, extended at the ends by her steeved bowsprit and boomkin; a big outboard rudder; a clipper bow; and a round-fronted cabin trunk which combines with a high coaming carried well aft. But for all the traditional detailing, the sail plan is a modern marconi rig of manageable size, in both the yawl and sloop versions. Here, too, it is a credit to Crocker's skill that he could set those sails on this hull and still keep it all in character.

More about this hull: Sallee Rover's scantlings are substantial for so small a vessel. Her keel, for example, is 7 x 9" oak; other structural members are sized accordingly. Crocker used the hull itself—particularly the heavy backbone—to ballast this boat, and thereby simplified construction by eliminating a ballast keel. Her down-low weight and wide body, plus some inside ballast and the sensible sail plan, make this a stiff boat in strong winds.

Her cockpit is self-bailing and the footwell is jogged, thus adding space and making good use of the coaming, cabin, and afterdeck for assorted seating under sail or at anchor. There are no below-deck accommodations shown, other than two transom berths with lockers under, and a platform for stowage forward of the mast— but the little cabin provides an airy and adequate shelter for camp-cruising. The recommended inboard auxiliary power is less than 10 hp and accessible through a large hatch in the cockpit sole.

She's special, Sallee Rover—a small wonder. She's the craft chosen to demonstrate, and celebrate, the anatomy of a wooden boat in a series of perspective drawings by Sam Manning for the 10th anniversary issue of *WoodenBoat* magazine (WB No. 60).

Six sheets of plans include lines and offsets, construction and sail plans for both the yawl and sloop versions, spars, wire rigging, tankage, and specifications. WB Plan No. 65. $150.00.

Plan 65

DESCRIPTION

Hull type: Round-bottomed, keel/cb boat
Rig: Marconi yawl or sloop
Construction: Carvel planked over steamed frames
Headroom/cabin (between beams): About 3'8"
Featured in Design Section: WB No. 62

PERFORMANCE

*Suitable for: Somewhat protected waters

*Intended capacity: 2–4 daysailing, 2 cruising
Trailerable: Yes
Propulsion: Sail w/inboard auxiliary
Speed (knots): 3–5

BUILDING DATA

Skill needed: Intermediate
Lofting required: Yes
*Alternative construction: Cold-molded, strip

PLANS DATA

No. of sheets: 6
Level of detail: Average
Cost per set: $150.00
WB Plan No. 65

See page 78 for further information.

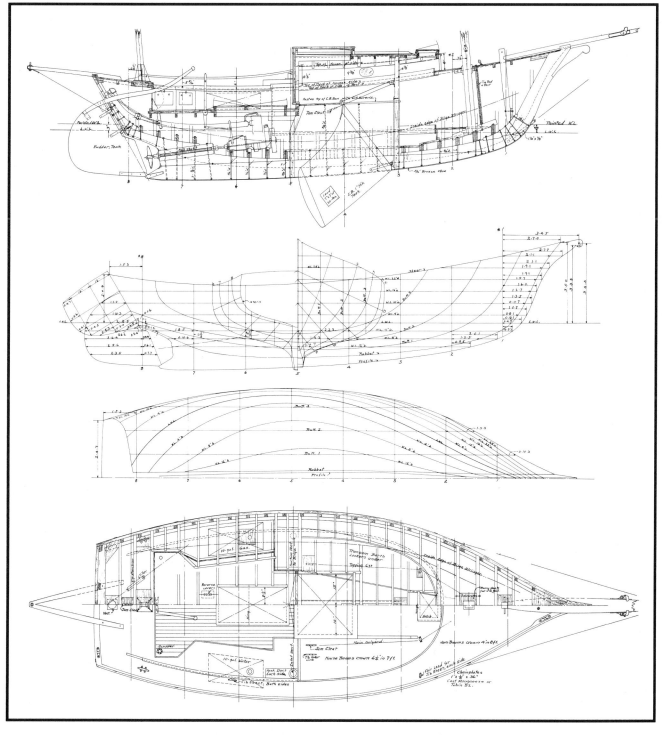

20′ Catboat, Madam Tirza

by Charles Wittholz

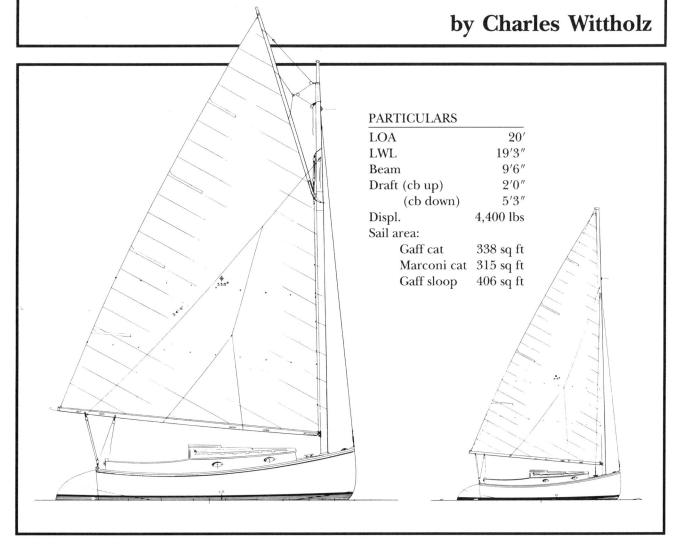

PARTICULARS	
LOA	20′
LWL	19′3″
Beam	9′6″
Draft (cb up)	2′0″
(cb down)	5′3″
Displ.	4,400 lbs
Sail area:	
Gaff cat	338 sq ft
Marconi cat	315 sq ft
Gaff sloop	406 sq ft

Madam Tirza, at 20′ overall, is the largest of the Wittholz-designed plywood catboats offered by WoodenBoat. Because she is bigger, she is less portable, but because of her size she has a longer range and makes a more versatile cruiser than her smaller sisters, featured in *Fifty Wooden Boats.*

Three sail plans are possible on this hull: a traditional gaff-rigged cat; a marconi cat; and, by adding a bowsprit, a gaff-rigged sloop with a self-tending jib. The first two rigs feature lazyjacks for ease of sail handling. Each of the three sail plans is fully detailed on separate sheets, including spars, blocks, running and standing rigging, fittings, and sails.

Once again, Wittholz offers the builder an optional outside ballast keel in place of the standard (and typical) centerboard with removable inside ballast. Construction, too, remains consistently straightforward and well presented, drawn with the home builder in mind: a V-bottomed hull built upside down over sawn frames that serve as station molds, and planked with panels of marine plywood.

Like Wittholz's 17′ cat, this boat has a centerline propeller protected by deadwood and a big outboard rudder. She has wheel steering; a 25-hp diesel is housed in a

low, raised motor hatch in the self-bailing cockpit. That cockpit offers sufficient space to daysail a small party, and accommodations below are anything but cramped. Being a catboat, Madam Tirza is by nature beamy; therefore, compared with other boats of this length, the room on board is everywhere remarkable—even with a centerboard trunk bisecting the cabin. The galley is divided, with a stove to port, a sink and icebox to starboard. A dropleaf table makes use of the trunk, on either side of which are settees. This boat, being the big sister, abounds with storage space—in cockpit lockers, a hanging locker in the cabin, drawers beneath the berths, shelves overhead, plus a broad forepeak. The toilet is located on the centerline and concealed beneath the forward end of the berths, directly below a hatch in the cabintop.

The careful detailing of this boat makes her an authentic Cape Cod cat in all respects but for a round-bottomed hull and perhaps a round-nosed house, both of which would add complexity to the construction with no appreciable gain in sailing ability or space onboard.

The plans for Madam Tirza are on eight sheets. In addition to four sheets of sail plans, there are lines and offsets, construction, the ballast keel, and arrangement plan. WB Plan No. 72. $95.00.

Plan 72

DESCRIPTION

Hull type: V-bottomed, centerboard (with optional keel)

Rig: Gaff or marconi cat; gaff sloop

Construction: Plywood planking over sawn frames

Headroom/cabin (between beams): About 4'6"

PERFORMANCE

*Suitable for: Somewhat protected waters

* *See page 78 for further information.*

*Intended capacity: 2–7 daysailing; 2 cruising

Trailerable: Yes; permit required

Propulsion: Sail w/inboard auxiliary

Speed (knots): 2–5

BUILDING DATA

Skill needed: Intermediate

Lofting required: Yes

*Alternative construction: None

PLANS DATA

No. of sheets: 8

Level of detail: Above average

Cost per set: $95.00

WB Plan No. 72

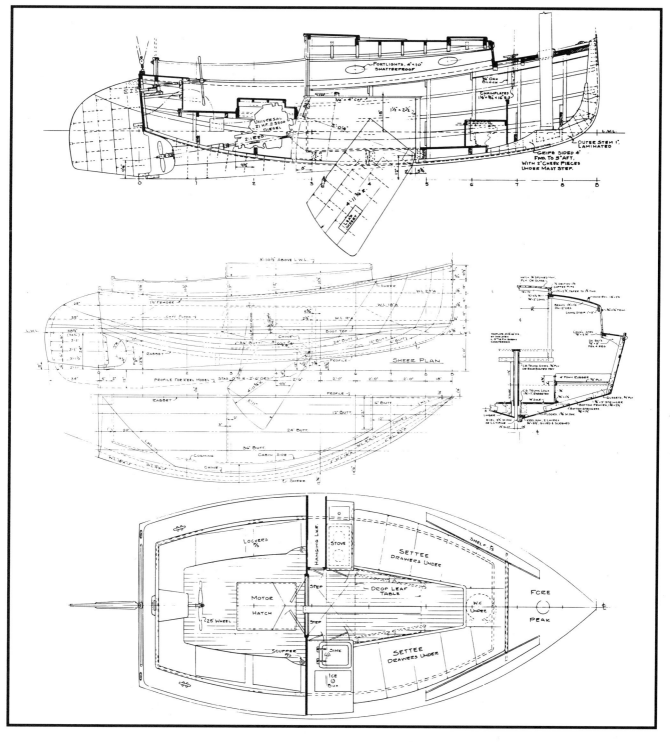

22'2" Sloop, Gray Seal

by Iain Oughtred

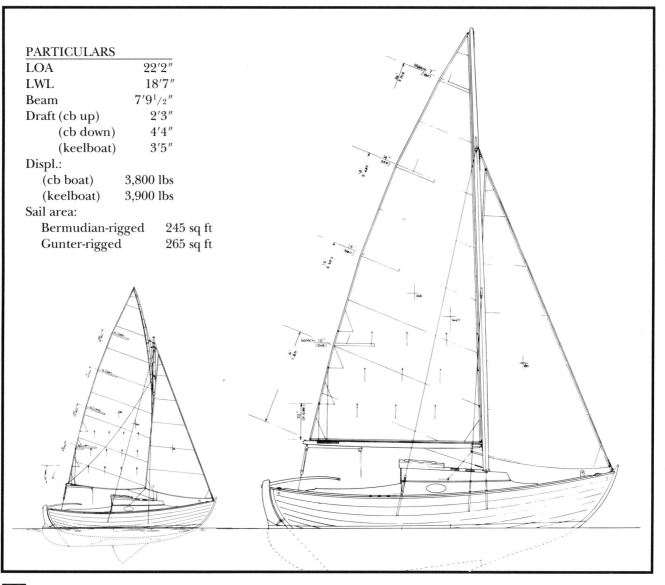

PARTICULARS		
LOA		22'2"
LWL		18'7"
Beam		7'9½"
Draft (cb up)		2'3"
(cb down)		4'4"
(keelboat)		3'5"
Displ.:		
(cb boat)	3,800 lbs	
(keelboat)	3,900 lbs	
Sail area:		
Bermudian-rigged	245 sq ft	
Gunter-rigged	265 sq ft	

This trailerable cruiser, drawn by Iain Oughtred, shows a subtle blend of Scandinavian characteristics. The strong sheer and very buoyant hull of the faering are combined with the low cabin of larger boats, such as the Tumlare and Cohoe. Rather than being a smaller version of these cruisers, this 22-footer is more what faering builders might produce if they wanted cruising accommodations.

Originally, Iain designed the keel/centerboard model to allow for easier trailering and broadened cruising grounds. But, realizing that many builders will prefer a deeper boat, he added the full-keeled version. Much to our pleasure, it looks rather like a small double-ended Folkboat.

The construction is suitable for amateur builders with some experience—or considerable patience and determination. Building techniques are essentially the same as for Iain's Acorn skiffs: epoxy-glued plywood planks on laminated frames and backbone. With proper care, these boats should last a long time.

Three basic layouts are shown, and combinations or variations of these are quite possible. A crew of two adults is ideal—two adults and two children represent, we think, the reasonable maximum.

Gray Seal's drawings (12 sheets) show details of deep-keeled and shoal-draft versions, and two rig options—gunter and jib-headed. Construction is well detailed, and Iain includes the critically important plank layout for the builder. Several construction elements are shown full scale. Owing to possible variations, interior joinery and engine installation are not drawn with great detail.

Gray Seal is a light, truly trailerable, cruiser. Although she goes together in contemporary fashion, she displays strong traditional character. WB Plan No. 91. $180.00.

Plan 91

DESCRIPTION

Hull type: Round-bottomed, outside-ballasted keel or keel/cb boat

Rig: Bermudian or gunter-rigged sloop

Construction: Lapstrake plywood over laminated frames

Headroom/cabin (between beams): About 4'6"

PERFORMANCE

*Suitable for: Somewhat protected waters (cb boat); open ocean (keelboat)

*See page 78 for further information.

*Intended capacity: 2–5 daysailing, 2–4 cruising

Trailerable: Yes

Propulsion: Sail

Speed (knots): 3–5

BUILDING DATA

Skill needed: Intermediate

Lofting required: Yes

*Alternative construction: Traditional plank on frame, strip, cold-molded

PLANS DATA

No. of sheets: 12

Level of detail: Above average

Cost per set: $180.00

WB Plan No. 91

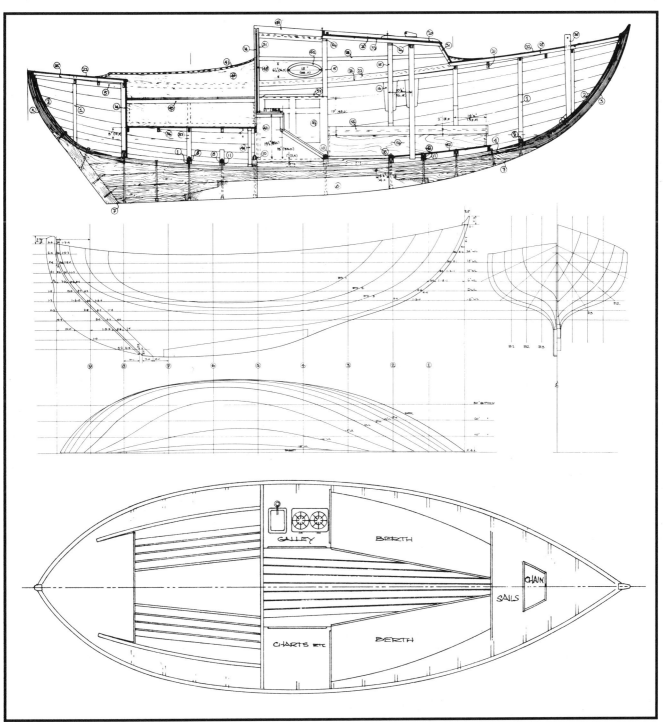

24′ Sloop, Amphibi-ette

by Mt. Desert Yacht Yard

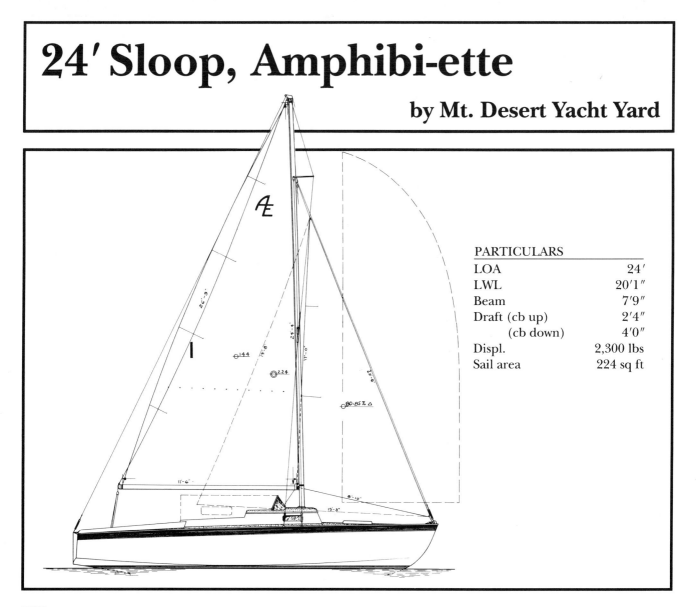

PARTICULARS	
LOA	24′
LWL	20′1″
Beam	7′9″
Draft (cb up)	2′4″
(cb down)	4′0″
Displ.	2,300 lbs
Sail area	224 sq ft

The Controversy line of yachts—the best known of which is the 25′ Amphibi-Con sloop—is as close as any shop came in wood to successfully competing with fiberglass in the postwar marketplace of production-built, family-sized sailboats.

As the name suggests, the Amphibi-ette is the Amphibi-Con made somewhat smaller. While the aesthetics of these boats may still be argued, the technology of their construction is no longer a subject of controversy, since the prototype was built and launched in 1951 at the Mt. Desert Yacht Yard in Maine. The boats in this line are similar in appearance but differ in size and detail. All of them have these features in common: light displacement, lots of room, manageable rigs, simplified construction, and speed under sail.

The Amphibi-ette, which appeared in the mid-'50s, is the most compact Controversy; her hull is unusual, even for this line. Topsides are marine-grade sheet plywood, and the bottom is strip-planked and shaped like an inverted bell. This bell bottom, in conjunction with a shallow keel housing the centerboard, serves several purposes: it concentrates weight and depth along the centerline and carries the chine farther outboard, thus lowering and widening the cabin sole for maximum room and headroom inside the boat.

At rest, the chine is clear of the waterline, and works as a roll damper; underway and with sufficient breeze, this hull can surf or plane downwind. Controversys make good use of bulkheads as hull reinforcement, similar to aircraft fuselage construction.

The reverse sheer and wide beam add space for more creature comfort within the boat. The Amphibi-ette's cockpit is self-bailing and offers ample seating area. The cabin has a canvas top, which can be rolled back to give unlimited headroom and visibility—weather permitting. In the main cabin there are transom berths on either side of the centerboard pedestal, which supports a small dining table. Going forward, the galley is to port, a hanging locker and additional stowage to starboard. The forward cabin contains two V-berths and the toilet, which is screened by the galley bulkhead. This area contains in addition a rope locker in the forepeak and is ventilated by a hatch in the foredeck—all this on a waterline length of 20′.

The Amphibi-ette's working sail area is only 224 sq ft, with a fractional rig and no running backstays. The mast is stepped and hinged on the cabin structure, which facilitates trailering and frees more space inside the cabin.

Plans for this boat are on six sheets: sail and arrangement plans, lines and offsets, construction, iron keel details, bulkheads, maststep and cockpit hood details. WB Plan No. 68. $125.00.

Plan 68

DESCRIPTION
Hull type: Inverted bell-bottom, light-displacement, keel/cb boat
Rig: Marconi sloop
Construction: Plywood topsides over bulkheads and stringers; strip-planked bottom
Headroom/cabin (between beams): About 4'6"
Featured in WB No. 61

PERFORMANCE
*Suitable for: Somewhat protected waters

* See page 78 for further information.

*Intended capacity: 4–6 daysailing, 4 cruising
Trailerable: Yes
Propulsion: Sail
Speed (knots): 3–6

BUILDING DATA
Skill needed: Intermediate
Lofting required: Yes
*Alternative construction: None

PLANS DATA
No. of sheets: 6
Level of detail: Average
Cost per set: $125.00
WB Plan No. 68

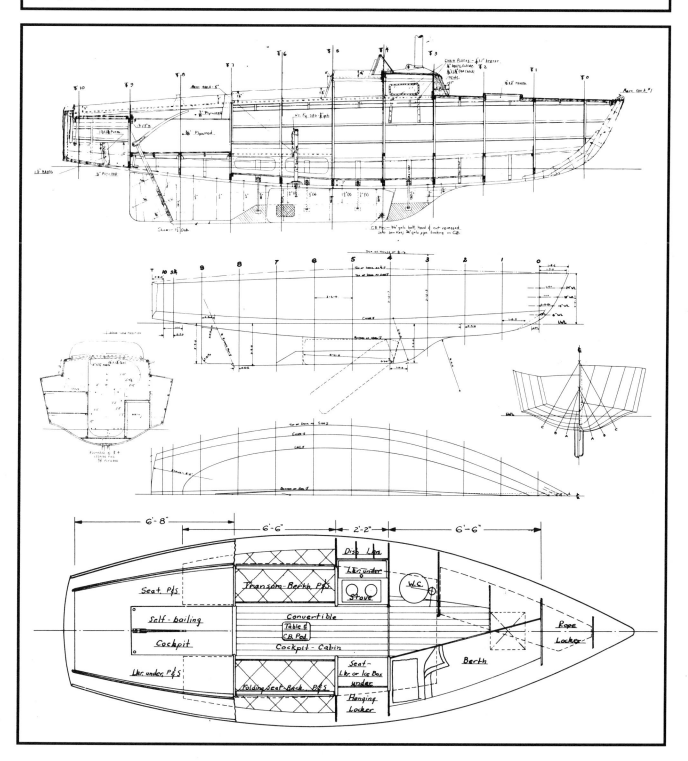

24'6" Sloop, Typhoon

by Winthrop Warner

PARTICULARS

LOA	24'6"
LWL	20'4"
Beam	9'
Draft	4'10"
Displ.	11,400 lbs
Sail area	376 sq ft

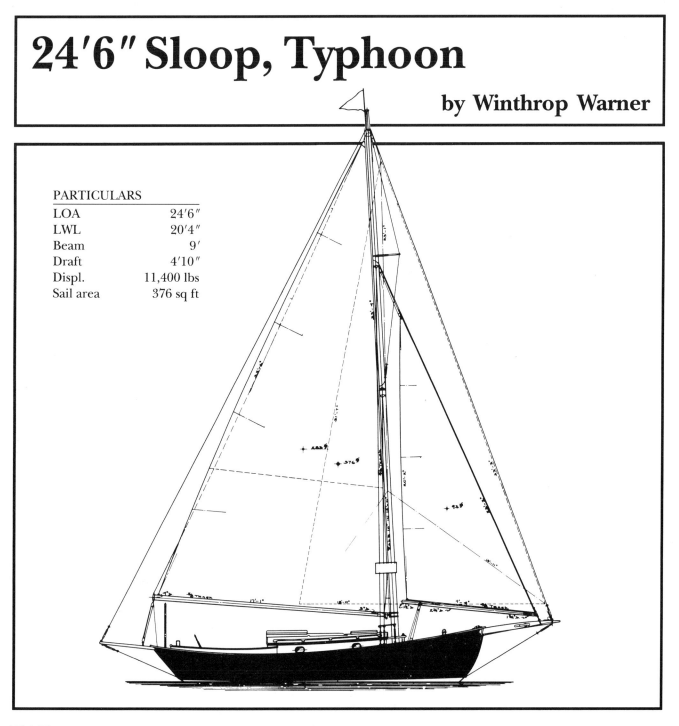

Winthrop Warner's formidable design reputation rests largely on his cruising yachts, which were designed to last, look good, and go long distances in solid comfort. Typhoon came off his drawing board in 1938; she is a roomy auxiliary sloop in a small package.

Her hull is deep and beamy, giving her—within the limits of her dimensions—considerable deck and cabin space, and enabling her to carry nearly 400 sq ft of working sail. The bowsprit and boomkin make this rig possible, and add a sweet line to the outboard profile—which Warner has enhanced with scrollwork, a capped bulwark, and a covestripe ending at the bow and stern. Note, too, some big-boat features: the boom gallows, the wheel steering, the sized-right, self-bailing cockpit, and the bridge deck, beneath which is housed a 25-hp auxiliary.

Construction is very husky throughout. In the cabin,

headroom is 5'. There are two berths forward with a toilet between them, and a convertible berth-dinette in the main cabin. On the port side is the galley with icebox, sink, stove, and generous stowage.

While not a large cruiser, Typhoon is fully appointed and equipped for offshore sailing. The three-fourths marconi rig is self-tending; a deep reef can be taken for heavy weather, and a lot more sail bent on for light air.

A second and quite different cabin arrangement plan was drawn, and built—indicating, at the least, the amount of space available in this hull in which to alter the interior. With either configuration, Typhoon can easily accommodate three adults.

The plans set for Typhoon consists of 11 sheets and includes: lines and offsets, construction, cabin arrangement, the alternate cabin arrangement, spars, scrollwork, and sail plan. WB Plan No. 64. $210.00.

Plan 64

DESCRIPTION

Hull type: Round-bottomed, outside-ballasted keelboat

Rig: Marconi sloop

Construction: Carvel planked over steamed frames

Headroom/cabin (between beams): About 5′

PERFORMANCE

*Suitable for: Open ocean

*See page 78 for further information.

*Intended capacity: 3–6 daysailing, 3 cruising

Trailerable: With difficulty, permit required

Propulsion: Sail w/inboard auxiliary

Speed (knots): 3–6

BUILDING DATA

Skill needed: Advanced

Lofting required: Yes

*Alternative construction: Cold-molded, strip

PLANS DATA

No. of sheets: 11

Level of detail: Above average

Cost per set: $210.00

WB Plan No. 64

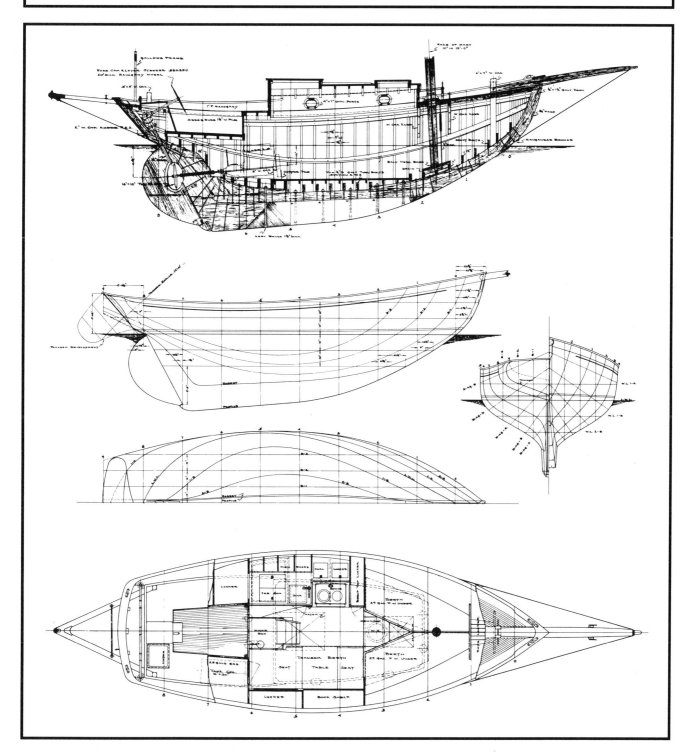

24'8" Skipjack, Calico Jack

by Joseph Gregory

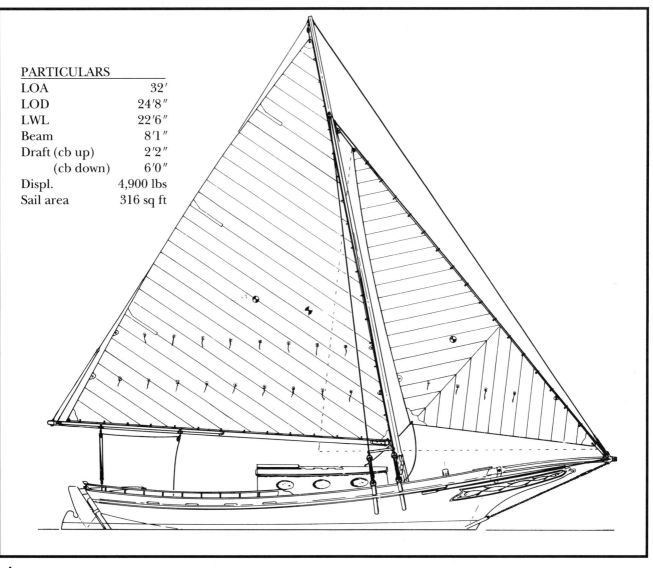

PARTICULARS	
LOA	32'
LOD	24'8"
LWL	22'6"
Beam	8'1"
Draft (cb up)	2'2"
(cb down)	6'0"
Displ.	4,900 lbs
Sail area	316 sq ft

A direct descendant of Chesapeake Bay's working skipjacks or two-sail bateaux, Calico Jack offers shoal-draft cruising for two and daysailing for a party—a big party. Designer Joe Gregory drew her for his own use after half a lifetime spent studying her relatives (for results from his survey of 45 working bateaux, see WB No. 79, page 110).

Calico Jack's rig might seem strange to modern eyes. Its almost comically low aspect ratio looks like it could have been pulled out of a bathtub toy or a cartoon in the Sunday paper, but it does provide considerable power for a minimum of heeling force. The mainsail forgives inattention and won't stall if slightly mistrimmed. A radically raked mast helps keep the boom clear of the water when reaching or running in a sea.

This little cruiser is rock stable and seldom needs her working jib, as the genoa can be carried in a 20-knot breeze. She seems at her best sailed a little free and heeled so her lee bottom parallels the water's surface.

Jack goes together Chesapeake fashion. Her bottom is cross planked with a staved forefoot (shaped from short, thick, vertical planks). This typical bateau construction makes good use of local materials and results in a clean interior because little framing is needed. (Note that the designer highly recommends Chapelle's *Boatbuilding* for an explanation of bateau construction.)

Deriving yachts from workboat origins involves a delicate balance. History has raised a select group of the resulting boats above their near sisters. Alden's Malabars, Stadel's Pilot Boats, Bolger's Light Dories, and a few others come to mind. Isolated technical arguments might be thrown at them, but taken as a whole they approach aesthetic perfection. Perhaps in her own simple way, Calico Jack is the same—among the best of her breed.

Seven sheets of plans include sail plan and arrangement, lines and offsets, two pages of construction detail and two pages of spar, fitting, and rigging details. WB Plan No. 74. $75.00.

Plan 74

DESCRIPTION

Hull type: V-bottomed centerboard
Rig: Skipjack
Construction: Traditional Chesapeake bateau
  construction
Headroom/cabin (between beams): About 4'
Featured in Design Section: WB No. 79

PERFORMANCE

*Suitable for: Somewhat protected waters

*See page 78 for further information.

*Intended capacity: 4–6 daysailing, 2 cruising
Trailerable: With difficulty
Propulsion: Sail
Speed (knots): 3–6

BUILDING DATA

Skill needed: Intermediate
Lofting required: Yes
*Alternative construction: None

PLANS DATA

No. of sheets: 7
Level of detail: Average
Cost per set: $75.00
WB Plan No. 74

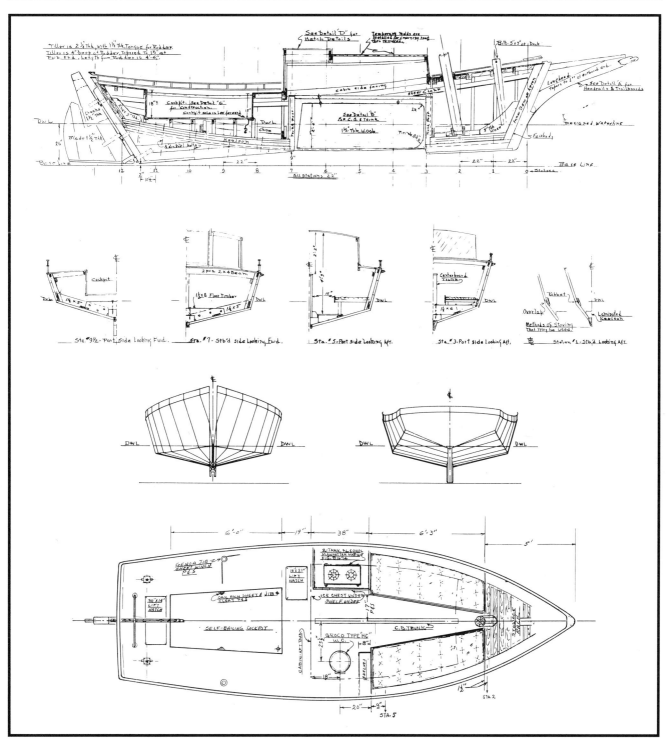

24'9" Canoe Yawl, Wenda

by Albert Strange

PARTICULARS	
LOA	24'9"
LWL	18'10"
Beam	6'4"
Draft (cb up)	2'2"
(cb down)	4'10"
Displ.	3,400 lbs
Sail area	273 sq ft

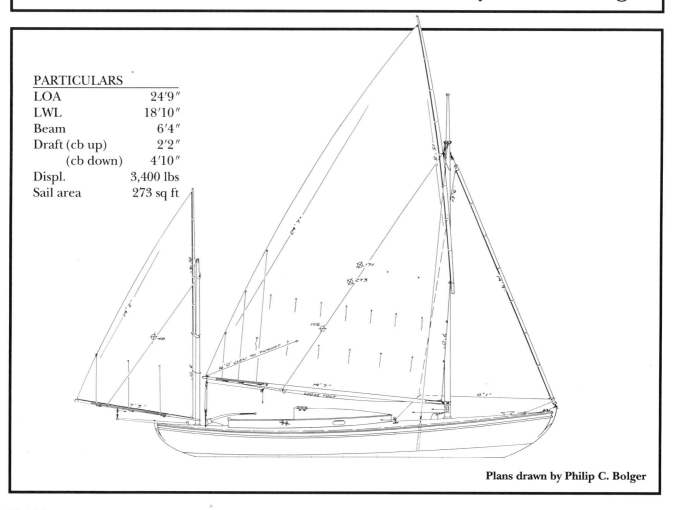

Plans drawn by Philip C. Bolger

Wenda will improve the scenery wherever she sails. Designed in the 19th century by artist Albert Strange, this romantic canoe yawl appeared in WB No. 80 (page 102). Response from experienced builders and sailors was immediate, positive, and passionate; but, much to our frustration, Wenda's complete plans did not exist. For help, we turned to noted contemporary designer Philip C. Bolger. An admirer of Strange's work, Phil responded with a truly striking set of drawings—and the following good words:

"Here is a significant design, necessary parts of which—including the lofting offsets—were missing. This is the fourth time I've had the assignment of filling in such blanks. The others were designs by respectable technicians of my own class of talent. I had no inhibitions about altering them whenever I thought of an improvement and the client approved.

"Albert Strange was something else again. He was a competent boat designer and draftsman, but he also had the indefinable flair that separates art from craft and made some of his work haunting. The memorable designs have to be treated with reverence and not tampered with. I've acted strictly as his draftsman here, as though I expected him to come in and inspect the tracings before signing his name to them.

"Wenda's hull form is as close to the surviving published tracing as I could make it, including deck and trunk. She is the slimmest and shallowest cruiser that Strange designed. Her shape is more adaptable to a wide range of construction methods, and 20th-century conditions, than his usual hollow-garboard models.

"No construction plan for this design is known. It's possible that there never was one, that she was intended for a builder who knew what to do and would have paid no attention to a construction plan if presented with one. I've made this one from other published Strange designs, following his practice, not my own. Strange was not much interested in construction. He did what was customary at the time. I see no reason for any builder to treat *this* drawing with deference; a U.S.-style carvel hull, a cold-molded shell, or even a lapstrake glued-plywood hull would all (I think) be acceptable to the shade of the master. The shape is very well suited to any of them. I find it surprising that she was not designed to be lapstrake, since that was the commonest method in England in her time. I suspect a class distinction—she is a canoe-*yacht*; yachts (for gentlemen) were smooth, whereas boats (for the commons) were clinker. If so, the distinction has become inverted with the passage of 90 years."

On four sheets of drawings, Bolger shows Wenda's sail plan and spar dimensions, lines and offsets, construction and arrangement, profile and section, and large-scale (1:8) construction sections. WB Plan No. 93. $60.00.

Plan 93

DESCRIPTION
Hull type: Round-bottomed, canoe-sterned
Rig: Lug-rigged yawl
Construction: Carvel planking over steamed frames
Headroom/cabin (between beams): About 3'8"
Featured in Design Section: WB No. 80
PERFORMANCE
*Suitable for: Somewhat protected waters
*Intended capacity: 2–4 daysailing, 2 cruising

*See page 78 for further information.

Trailerable: With difficulty
Propulsion: Sail
Speed (knots): 3–6
BUILDING DATA
Skill needed: Advanced
Lofting required: Yes
*Alternative construction: Cold-molded, lapstrake
  plywood
PLANS DATA
No. of sheets: 4
Level of detail: Average
Cost per set: $60.00
WB Plan No. 93

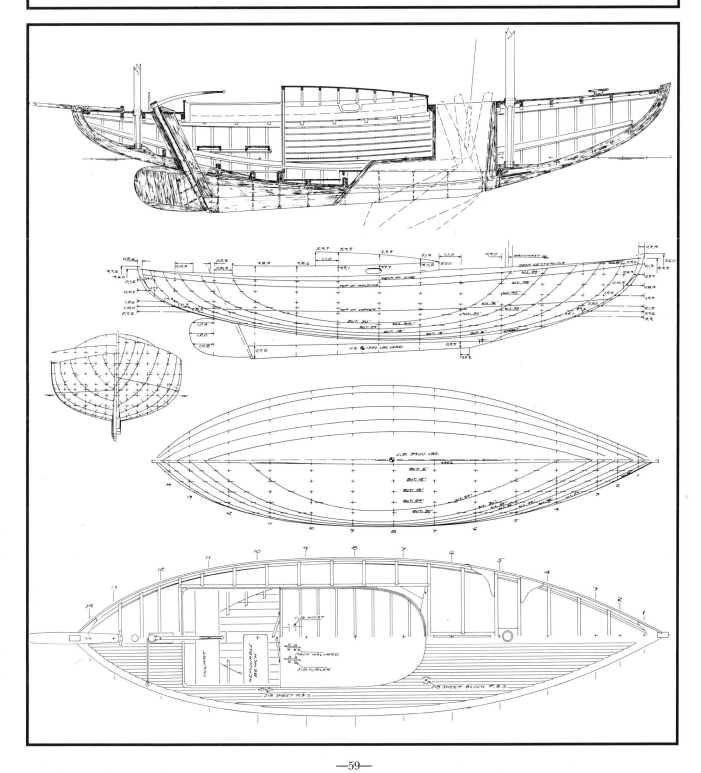

27'6" Sloop, Controversy 27

by Mt. Desert Yacht Yard

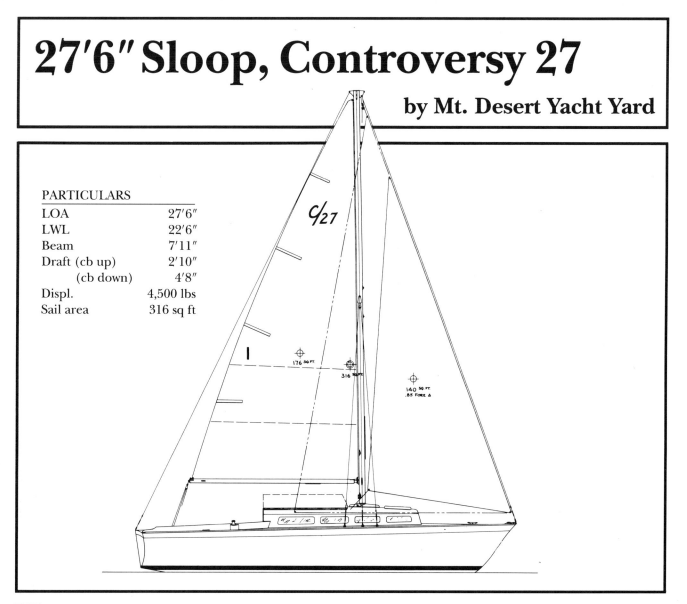

PARTICULARS

LOA	27'6"
LWL	22'6"
Beam	7'11"
Draft (cb up)	2'10"
(cb down)	4'8"
Displ.	4,500 lbs
Sail area	316 sq ft

The Controversy 27 was intended to refine and re-place the most popular of the Controversys, the Amphibi-Con. The 27 has a built-down keel (the Amphibi-Con had a fin); a straight sheer (the Amphibi-Con, a less-attractive reverse); a masthead rig (the Amphibi-Con, a seven-eighths rig); and is more boat in the water (the Amphibi-Con is 2' shorter overall).

Fiberglass took the country by storm before the C/27 could make her mark. It's unfortunate that this design didn't become more popular, because there's sound thinking behind her development. For example: the hull is shaped to provide a narrow bilge beneath the cabin sole for the containment of bilgewater with the boat heeled; the cockpit seats are long enough to serve as berths for two people; and the masthead rig is efficient and simpler to set up.

Like the Amphibi-Con before her, the C/27 has a round-bottomed, strip-planked hull, utilizing a series of strategically placed bulkheads to give it form and strength. Light weight, shoal draft, and a tabernacled mast make the C/27 a portable cruiser, trailerable be-hind the family car. No boatyard is necessary, even with almost 28' of boat here.

Her centerboard is contained entirely within the ballast keel, so there is no trunk to crowd the cabin. The pedestal for the centerboard serves as a little table;

it converts to a larger, dining table when needed.

Because displacement is light and the hull fast, a small outboard is adequate auxiliary power. This is kept in a motorwell behind a watertight bulkhead at the after end of the cockpit, and is accessible through two hatches. Al-ternatively, an inboard engine can be installed beneath the cockpit, in which case the lazarette houses most of the exhaust system.

If the Amphibi-Con's primary selling point was her spacious interior, then the C/27 made a good thing bet-ter. Not counting the berths for two in the cockpit, the cabin can comfortably accommodate four people. Light-ing, lockers, stowage, ventilation, seating, privacy—they're all here in extra measure. And, as in her smaller sisters in the Controversy line, standing headroom is achieved in the main cabin and galley by means of a long, large hatch with an adjustable canvas hood.

The C/27 is faster, more maneuverable, and better balanced than many boats in her size range; as she is a light-displacement craft, her rig and gear are downsized and easier to handle.

Drawn in 1960, the plans for this smart sailer/cruiser include lines and offsets, sails and spars, construction, lead or iron keel, arrangement and deck plan. An addi-tional 37 drawings provide details for rigging, fittings, and joinerwork. WB Plan No. 69. $150.00.

Plan 69

DESCRIPTION
Hull type: Round-bottomed, light-displacement,
   keel/cb boat
Rig: Marconi sloop
Construction: Strip-planked over bulkhead/frames
Headroom/cabin (between beams): About 5′2″;
   6′2″ with canvas hood
Featured in WB No. 61

PERFORMANCE
*Suitable for: Somewhat protected waters

* *See page 78 for further information.*

*Intended capacity: 6–8 daysailing, 4–6 cruising
Trailerable: Yes
Propulsion: Sail w/auxiliary outboard
Speed (knots): 3–6

BUILDING DATA
Skill needed: Intermediate
Lofting required: Yes
*Alternative construction: None

PLANS DATA
No. of sheets: 8
Level of detail: Above average
Cost per set: $150.00
WB Plan No. 69

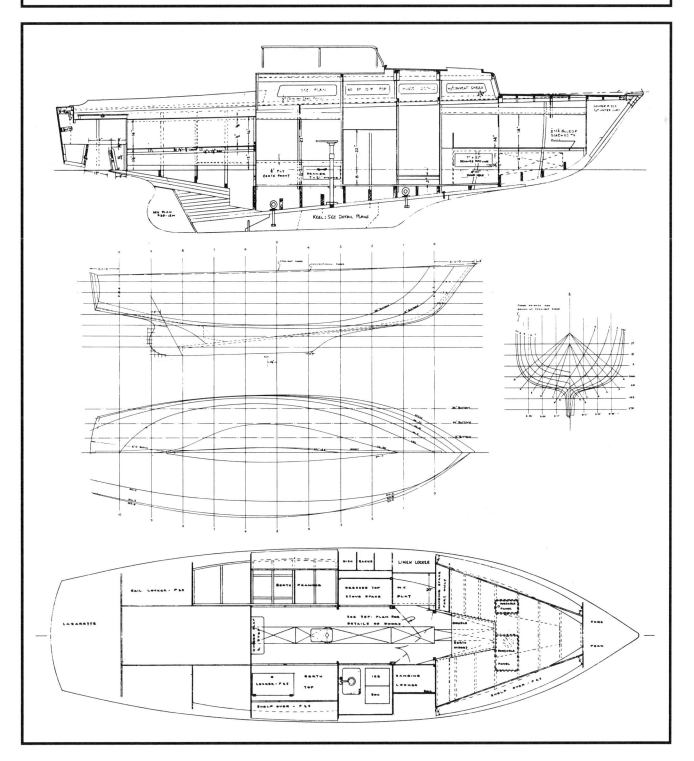

27'9" Cutter, Capt. Blackburn

by William Garden

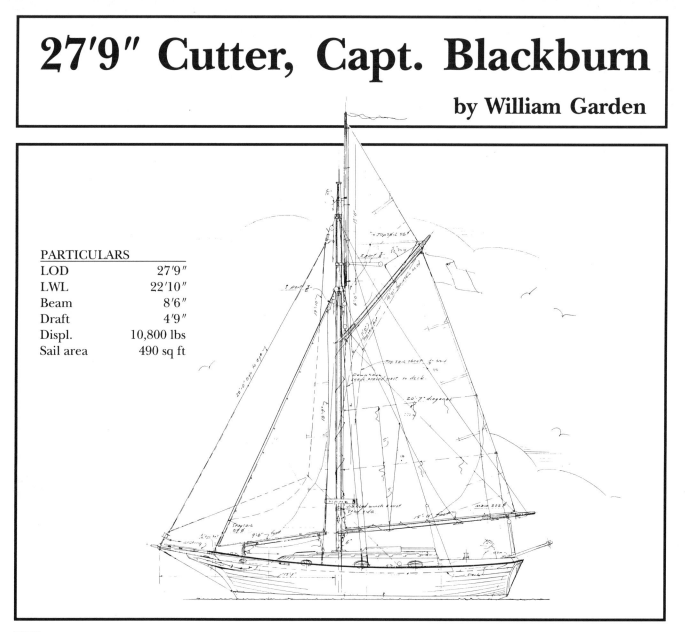

PARTICULARS

LOD	27'9"
LWL	22'10"
Beam	8'6"
Draft	4'9"
Displ.	10,800 lbs
Sail area	490 sq ft

This cruising cutter by William Garden is based on his close study of a similar vessel that made an epic transatlantic crossing from New England to Old England in 1899. Garden has honored, by name, that vessel's owner and skipper—Capt. Howard Blackburn, whose voyage made history because he singlehanded it in 61 days—without fingers or toes, having lost all digits as a Grand Banks doryman some years before.

Garden's boat is modeled after Blackburn's, though not a replica. The designer departs sufficiently from the original boat to make his version a small but substantial family yacht, dimensioned less than 28' on deck. Alternatively, the boat can be viewed and used as a sized-right, long-distance singlehander for the mariner so inclined.

To meet varied requirements like that—and to meet, in any case, the rigorous demands of offshore work—takes not just a good design but skilled construction. Garden has quite literally built this boat on paper in masterfully drafted detail. His signature style of architectural graphics is of immeasurable assistance for those who wish to raise these drawings into three dimensions.

Garden's Blackburn features a deep ballast keel, a tall bulwark, tiller steering, and a long, low cabin that houses all the amenities below. The cockpit is comparatively brief, as befits a seaboat, and is protected by a high coaming. Auxiliary power is provided by a small diesel that works through a reduction gear to give five knots in flat water.

The working lower sails are all inboard and are virtually self-tending; for light weather, the jib and topsail can be handily added (or subtracted, if the wind breezes up) without endangering the crew or fouling the rig. The resulting sail plan is manageable, adjustable, and takes advantage of improved deck gear.

Hull construction, like the rig, is more modern than first meets the eye. She is cold-molded, and Garden has drawn the setup for this method just as you would see it on the building floor.

Capt. Blackburn is a compact, heavy-duty, character cruiser with a wealth of fine touches—clipper bow, gaff rig, light boards, and a davit-slung skiff. She's loaded. The fitting reward for completing a boat of this caliber and complexity is the open ocean itself.

Plans consist of 11 sheets: lines and offsets, sail plan, arrangement, cabin and construction sections, keel and construction plan, deck framing and hold (plumbing and mechanical), and four sheets covering hardware, rig, and miscellaneous details. WB Plan No. 78. $150.00.

Plan 78

DESCRIPTION
Hull type: Round-bottomed keelboat
Rig: Gaff cutter
Construction: Cold-molded
Headroom/cabin (between beams): About 5′9″
PERFORMANCE
*Suitable for: Open ocean
*Intended capacity: 3–8 daysailing, 4 cruising

*See page 78 for further information.

Trailerable: With difficulty; permit required
Propulsion: Sail w/auxiliary inboard engine
Speed (knots): 3–6
BUILDING DATA
Skill needed: Advanced
Lofting required: Yes
*Alternative construction: Carvel, strip
PLANS DATA
No. of sheets: 11
Level of detail: Above average
Cost per set: $150.00
WB Plan No. 78

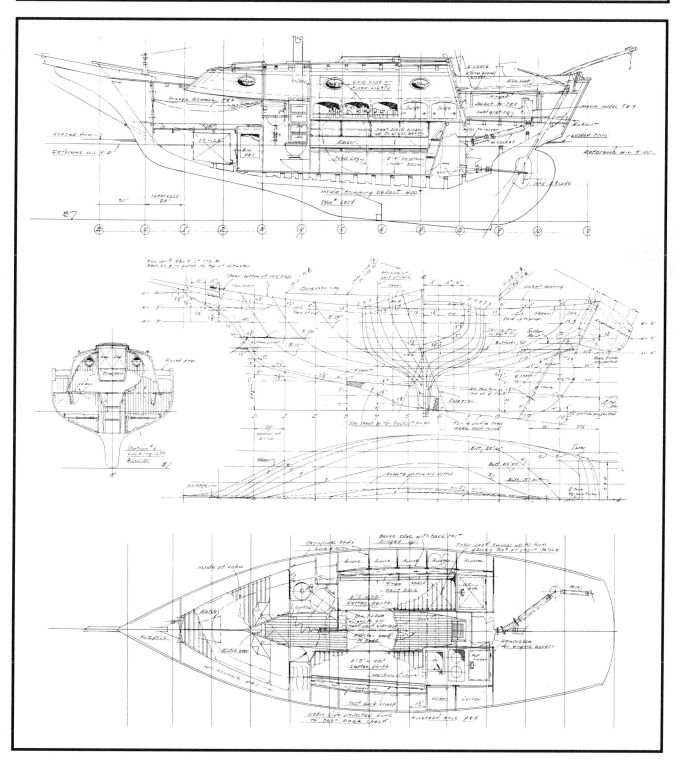

29′ Cutter

by Paul Gartside

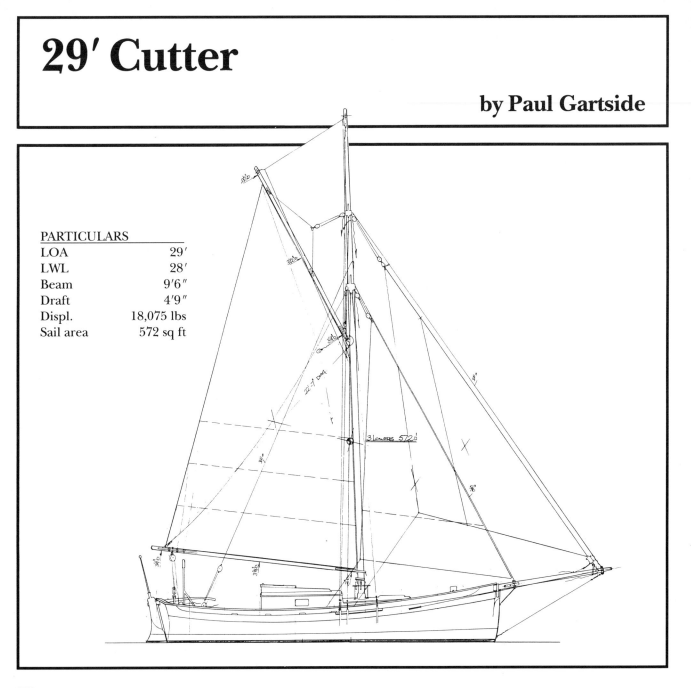

PARTICULARS

LOA	29′
LWL	28′
Beam	9′6″
Draft	4′9″
Displ.	18,075 lbs
Sail area	572 sq ft

Paul Gartside is a yacht builder and designer whose standards of excellence in both areas are evident in this 29′ auxiliary cutter. Quite often, builders who put designs on paper omit critical aspects of finish or construction, because they are accustomed to supplying their own. The drawings for this Gartside cutter are nicely detailed; all the pertinent information is clearly presented so the design can be fully realized on the building floor.

The design itself is decidedly a deep-sea, deep-keel boat, built and ballasted to go offshore comfortably and return safely. She is a 20th-century cruising yacht reminiscent of the best of 19th-century English and American working sail. This cutter carries over three tons of either lead or iron outside ballast, displaces 9 tons, and draws nearly 5′ of water. In keeping with her seagoing abilities, the two-tier, low-profile cabin is protected by bulwarks; the cockpit is a footwell to minimize the flooded volume if filled with water; and the steering is simply a tiller controlling an outboard rudder, a reliable system favored by many blue-water sailors.

This cutter has generous accommodations for four in a naturally lighted, sensibly arranged, straightforward interior that is unusually roomy for a boat of this overall length, thanks to her full sections and long waterline. Other distinctive features include: a radiused transom (with guidelines from the designer to assist lofting); copper-riveted carvel planking over doubled, steamed frames (rivets for greater holding power, and laminated timbers for easier bending); custom hardware of painted aluminum or galvanized mild steel (for affordable fabrication and for an authentic appearance).

Unlike some production boats wearing pin rails and boom gallows, as if these items were fashion accessories, Gartside's cutter is the genuine article—an absolutely salty craft throughout, where all the gear serves a real purpose and the detailing is appropriate to this smart tops'l gaffer that looks like she can sail across time. Plans are on five sheets: lines, layout and sections, sail, construction, offsets, and building setup. WB Plan No. 84. $150.00.

Plan 84

DESCRIPTION

Hull type: Round-bottomed, outside-ballasted keel boat

Rig: Cutter

Construction: Carvel-planked over laminated frames

Headroom/cabin (between beams): About 6′1″

PERFORMANCE

*Suitable for: Open ocean

*See page 78 for further information.

*Intended capacity: 3–8 daysailing, 4–5 cruising

Trailerable: With difficulty; permit required

Propulsion: Sail w/auxiliary

Speed (knots): 3–7

BUILDING DATA

Skill needed: Advanced

Lofting required: Yes

*Alternative construction: Cold-molded, strip

PLANS DATA

No. of sheets: 5

Level of detail: Average

Cost per set: $150.00

WB Plan No. 84

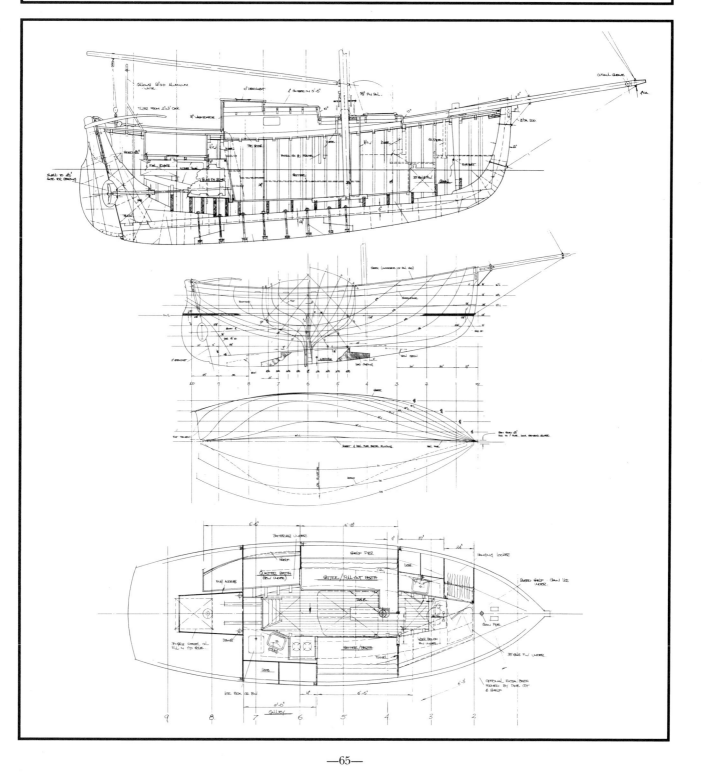

37'3" Yawl, Controversy 36

by Mt. Desert Yacht Yard

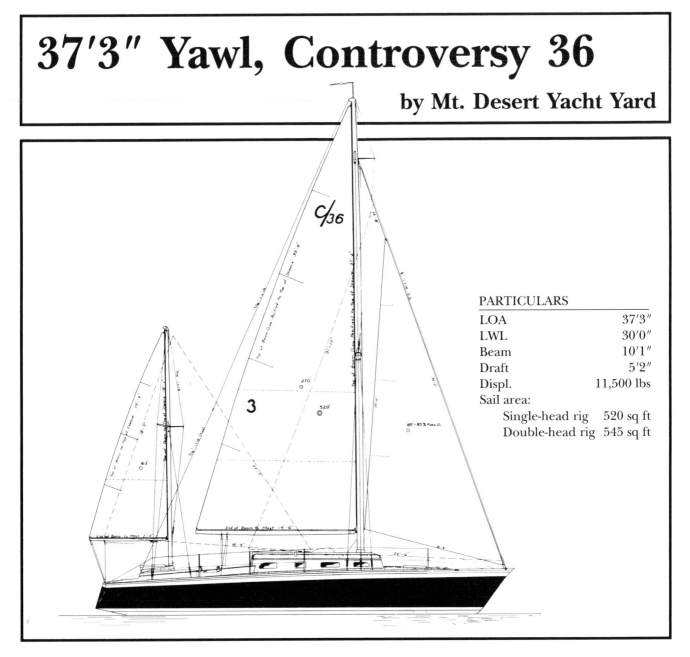

PARTICULARS	
LOA	37'3"
LWL	30'0"
Beam	10'1"
Draft	5'2"
Displ.	11,500 lbs
Sail area:	
Single-head rig	520 sq ft
Double-head rig	545 sq ft

Here is the ultimate development of the Amphibi-Con and the top of the Controversy line of yachts. The 36 is actually over 37' long and was given both single- and double-headed yawl configurations. Her comparatively light displacement (a feature of all the Controversys) enables this boat to be powered by a small auxiliary inboard, with a small sail plan, and handled with light gear—and frequently sailed singlehanded, despite her size. One of these boats, built with a modified deck-and-cabin plan, made a successful circumnavigation.

While the Controversy construction system and high-sheer hull form combine to give this line of boats more room below deck than other sailing craft of similar dimensions, the accommodations aboard the C/36 are exceptional by any measurement. The standard arrangement plan has two quarter berths, a double berth, one or two singles, a large enclosed head, and a generous galley. Seven people can sit in comfort around the cabin table.

In addition, there is an aft cabin that sleeps two and has its own small cockpit. Besides the 'midship cockpit, which is capacious, there is a third, smaller cockpit in the bow—for handling ground tackle, or sails, or for simply enjoying the view. Throughout this boat there is an expansive sense of space, thanks to wide floors, high headroom, and lots of natural light.

The C/36 has the typical Controversy hull construction: strip planks glued to permanent bulkheads or laminated members, with the interior joinerwork doubling as a structural element. The result is a light but rigid yacht, whose modern lines have given her a reputation as a fast sailer. A 25-hp gas engine can easily push this hull to 7$\frac{1}{2}$ knots.

We have become accustomed, nowadays, to light-displacement sailboats: they're routinely campaigned as ocean racers or marketed as racer-cruisers—all of which tends to vindicate a boat like the Controversy 36, introduced over 25 years ago. She's still an uncommon craft, but no longer an anomaly on the water.

E. Farnham Butler and Cyrus Hamlin collaborated on the design and engineering of the Controversy line. Plans for the C/36 are on 16 sheets, which include sail plans for the two yawl rigs, lines and offsets, construction details, spars, keel, arrangement, rigging, and mast-fitting details. WB Plan No. 70. $300.00.

Plan 70

DESCRIPTION

Hull type: Round-bottomed, outside-ballasted keelboat

Rig: Marconi yawl with single or double headsails

Construction: Strip-planked over bulkheads and frames

Headroom/cabin (between beams): About 6′3″

Featured in WB No. 61

PERFORMANCE

*Suitable for: Open ocean

*See page 78 for further information.

*Intended capacity: 6–8 daysailing, 6–7 cruising

Trailerable: No

Propulsion: Sail w/inboard auxiliary

Speed (knots): 3–7

BUILDING DATA

Skill needed: Intermediate to advanced

Lofting required: Yes

*Alternative construction: None

PLANS DATA

No. of sheets: 16

Level of detail: Above average

Cost per set: $300.00

WB Plan No. 70

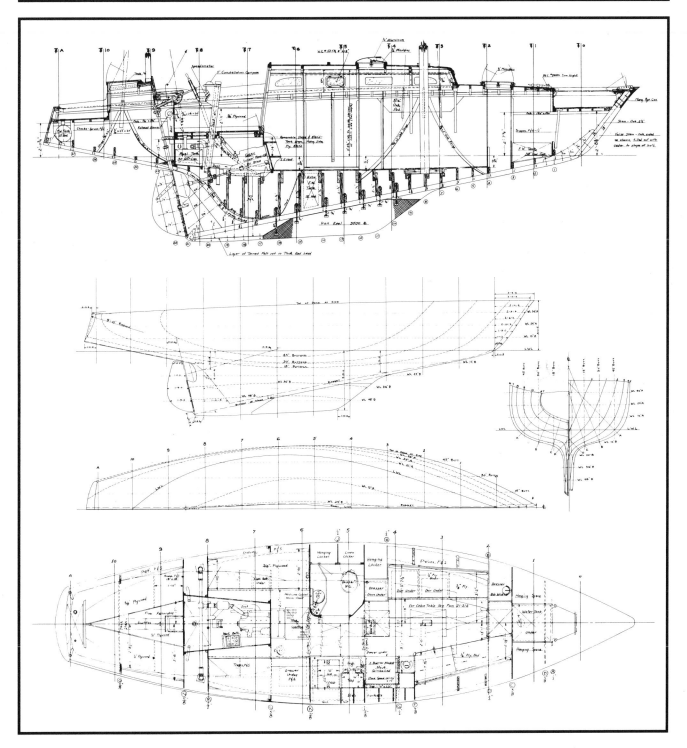

Other related products from the

WoodenBoat Merchandise Catalog

FIFTY WOODEN BOATS: A Catalog of Building Plans

by WoodenBoat Magazine
112 pg., illustrated, softcover
Product #325–060
$11.95

If you haven't yet found a boat which meets all your requirements, our first catalog of plans contains information on 50 more designs! Full-sized construction plans for each of our scale models are described—as are designs for sliding-seat rowing shells, sharpies, schooners, daysailers, and cruising boats. Included are designs by John Alden, Concordia Company, Fenwick Williams, Ralph Munroe, and Uffa Fox—as well as others by Charles Wittholz, Joel White, and Nelson Zimmer. Our first catalog is just as informative as *Thirty Wooden Boats*, with each design fully described and illustrated.

THE RUNABOUT POSTER

If the Gentleman's Runabout on pages 36 and 37 of this catalog has caught your eye, this full-color poster by Stephen L. Davis will undoubtedly convince you to build it! With drawings of the 28′ Hacker-designed IRENE, Davis beautifully illustrates construction and finish details common to both of these craft. Complemented by a rich sienna brown border, the poster is on high-quality, heavy paper and measures 26″ x 23″ overall. *Product #710–011* **$11.95**

THE WOODEN BOAT POSTER

This series of perspective drawings was done by Samuel F. Manning, a marine artist and technical illustrator well known to *WoodenBoat* readers. His subject is the Crocker-designed yawl Sallee Rover, whose plans are featured on pages 46 and 47 of this catalog. The drawings are printed on a cream background with dark-brown lines work and lettering and muted red accents. Overall size: $17^1/_2$″ x 26″. *Product #710–008* **$11.95**

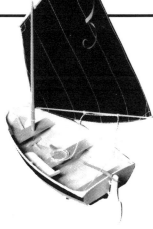

NUTSHELL PRAM MODEL

Based on the 7′7″ Nutshell Pram designed by Joel White, this V-bottomed model has a single 'midship frame, glued lapstrake topsides, and sheet-planked ends and bottom. Daggerboard trunk, rudder, tiller, and tanbark sail (material included) add character and authenticity. You provide the streamer! *Product #620–001W* **$39.95**

YANKEE TENDER MODEL

Built like the 12′4″ flat-bottomed Yankee Tender skiff, this model features lapstrake planking and a cross-planked bottom. An easy model to build, it's just the right boat for practicing lapstrake planking at a manageable size. *Product #620–002W* **$49.95**

TWO GREAT SOURCES FOR INFORMATION ON WOODEN BOATS AND RELATED ITEMS

Request our Merchandise catalog to see all of the plans, tools, kits, clothing, books, videos, and AudioBooks we offer. Request our WoodenBoat School catalog to read about the courses we offer for a hands-on experience in learning the art of building, rigging, or sailing a wooden boat. For free catalogs, write to either WoodenBoat School or WoodenBoat Merchandise. P.O. Box 78, Brooklin, Maine 04616; or call 1–800–225–5205.

Continued from page 7

Stability

The ability of a boat to stand up to its spread of sail against a heavy breeze results from many factors: hull shape, beam, draft, displacement, amount of ballast and where it is placed, size and height of the sail plan, the weight of its spars, and even the onboard location of its crew. But the basics of stability can be shown rather neatly in a simple illustration (Figure 7).

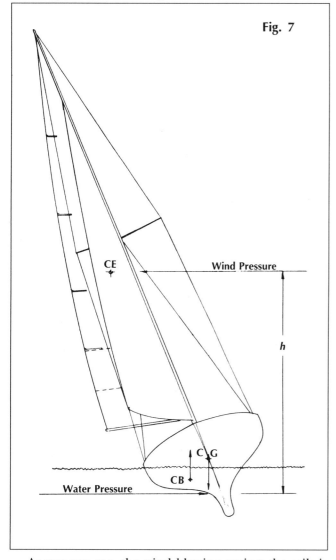

Fig. 7

CE

Wind Pressure

h

C G

CB

Water Pressure

As you can see, the wind blowing against the sails is resisted by the water pressure against the underbody, the two forces being separated by the vertical distance *h*. This resulting twist tends to heel the boat, as well as move her forward through the water. Resisting and offsetting this so-called heeling moment is the so-called righting moment caused by the buoyancy of the hull (a force which acts upwards at the heeled center of buoyancy) and the downward force of the boat's weight located at its center of gravity. The distance separating the opposing forces of buoyancy and gravity is the righting arm which we will call *a*, and the righting moment is equal to the displacement of the boat times the righting arm *a*: Righting moment = (displacement x *a*) expressed in foot-pounds. This is pretty much how naval architects actually calculate the real stability of a design, using a little jiggery-pokery to account for heeled hull shape, cosines of heel angle, and table of wind pressures per square foot of sail area.

But for now we are interested only in your understanding the concept of boat stability, and how to judge whether a design will be stiff or tender. As you can see from Figure 7, anything that will increase the righting moment will improve stability—more displacement, or an increased righting arm because of a lower center of gravity, or wider, harder bilges. Anything reducing the righting moment or increasing the heeling moment will worsen stability—in the first instance, perhaps, a higher center of gravity or slack bilges; in the second instance, more sail area or a higher center of effort. So even a casual inspection of a design can give you some clues about its stability. A narrow boat with inside ballast and a large sail plan may be suspected of too little stability. A wide, heavy fin-keeler with lots of ballast will likely be very stiff, and able to stand up to a large sail area. Small boats rely a good deal on the weight of their crew on the windward rail to provide stability (a lateral shift in the center of gravity), but there is an unfortunate trend in some of the most modern small ocean racers to depend on this as a stabilizing force. There have been some accidents already, and probably there will be more. Live ballast is perfectly feasible in short, inshore races, but to depend on crew weight to keep a boat upright on longer offshore races strikes me as folly. Crews get tired and seasick, and their agility and judgment suffer as a result.

Perhaps the most important aspect of stability is its range—at what heel angle does the righting arm stop increasing and start to decrease, and at what heel angle does it become zero, and then negative, causing a sure capsize? A recent study of sailboat stability at sea, aimed at reducing accidents in ocean races, discovered that an alarming number of boats, even though stable to a 90° knockdown, will, if rolled completely upside down (180°), remain that way, with their masts pointing down and ballast keels waving in the air. Figure 8 shows how this is possible, although, because of dynamic forces caused by large waves and gale-force winds, the true situation is much more complex. What often seems to happen is that the boat will remain upside down for a considerable period of time, until a breaking sea rolls her back to nearly 90°, when normal righting forces will return her to upright.

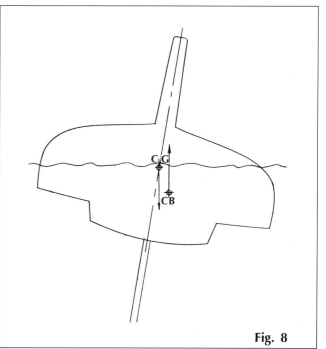

C G

CB

Fig. 8

The calculations necessary to arrive at a plot of righting arm against heel angle are more complex and time consuming. But some generalities can be made. Wide, shoal hulls, such as centerboard daysailers or catamarans, have a lot of stability at low heel angles, but will become unstable at 45–90°, and capsize when the righting arm becomes zero and goes negative. Deep, heavy cruisers with lots of outside ballast will have a much greater range of stability, and will be able to right themselves if heeled beyond 90°, some even to 180° (see Figure 9). Stability is a desirable thing in any boat, and is an important consideration in any design. This is not to say that non-self-righting boats are undesirable and to be avoided—quite the contrary. Probably the majority of boats sailing have a stability limit of 90° or less—all the Beetle Cats, Snipes, Lightnings, prams, peapods, and catamarans that so many of us sail fall into this category. They are wonderful boats for the normal conditions in which they are used, and when sailed with understanding are safe and forgiving.

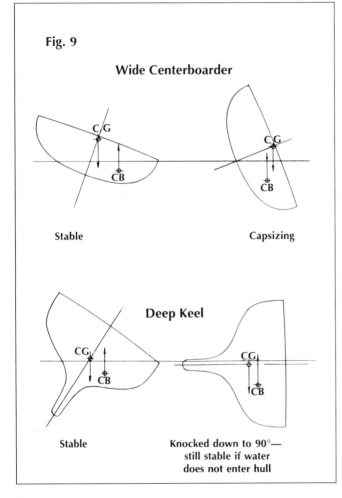

Fig. 9

Wide Centerboarder

C/G   C/G
CB   CB

Stable   Capsizing

Deep Keel

CG   CG
CB   CB

Stable   Knocked down to 90°—
                still stable if water
                does not enter hull

Accommodations

Accommodations plans are always interesting to study. Perhaps nothing requires more time and concentration from the designer than the puzzle of fitting comfortable, workable living quarters into the oddly shaped, cramped inside of a boat hull. The smaller the boat, the more difficult the job of planning the interior. Headroom, footroom, and elbow room have to be fought for; like baseball, it is a game of inches.

When studying the accommodations plan of a design for the first time, start by getting a feel for the floor area. Unlike a house, with vertical walls and floor area the same size as the rooms, a small boat hull becomes narrower toward the bottom, and the space available for the cabin sole is necessarily narrow. Most designers show this floor area on the accommodations plan. Try to find this and understand how much standing space is available in various parts of the boat. The cabin sole, as this floor is called, is usually widest amidships and tapers in width as one goes forward or aft. Try also to visualize what the traffic patterns below will be, and whether or not the restrictions in floor space will allow for the expected traffic without bottlenecks. Does the cook have to stand in the only passageway fore and aft, or can the traffic bypass the galley without interference? Spaces such as toilet rooms, which are often off-center, usually suffer from restricted footroom and may become difficult to use. The toilet normally is raised up on a platform higher than the floor, and the location of the attendant seacocks also cuts into the available floor space.

Along with the restricted floor space, most small craft have headroom in only a portion of the interior. Ordinarily, the outline of the cabin trunk delineates the extent of the full headroom that is available below. This is usually shown as a dot-and-dash line on the plan view of the cabin layout. Find the outline of the trunk on the accommodations plan, and visualize what this means to the traffic below and the space that is available for various activities. Does the forward cabin have full headroom, or must you crouch? Can you stand upright in the shower? If the design calls for an off-center passageway between the main cabin and an aft cabin, does it have a slanted floor, as well as restricted headroom? If so, this can be difficult to negotiate in rough weather. The space outboard of the cabin trunk, under the side decks, will have much less overhead space and must be used for functions which do not require headroom. The designer should have included some joiner sections with the accommodations plan— cross sections through the hull at various locations showing the joinerwork arrangement and layout. These are a big help in your visualization of the interior, and the space—or lack of it—available for each function.

Accommodations should be planned according to intended use of the boat. The arrangement of a 40-footer intended for ocean passages and long cruises would be quite different from the same boat's interior laid out for marina liveaboards. It is important to understand the intended use of the boat before critiquing the layout. Headroom and floor space are less important to the racer than they are to the cruising man.

A careful analysis of a cabin layout should take into account the foreward and after locations of the various elements. You are all aware that the forward one-third of a boat hull suffers most from severe motion and noise when in rough water, while the middle and after sections are less jumpy and noisy. These considerations should be taken into account when planning interiors that must function offshore. Galleys that are located aft are always more tenable, and can be better ventilated, which can sometimes make the difference between getting a hot meal or getting none at all. Bunks located in the forepeak don't get much use in offshore boats, while a big double bunk in the forward cabin is a nice arrangement for the liveaboard couple at the marina.

Try to get a feel for the available stowage space in relation to the number of bunks. There is a tendency nowadays to crowd in a lot of bunks and, as a result, locker and shelf space suffer. Again, it boils down to the intended use. The racing skipper needs a lot of bunks for his crew, and can tolerate less comfort, while the cruising man will want fewer bunks and more comfort and stowage.

Aesthetics

The aesthetic aspects of boat design are so subjective, and vary so much from one person to another, that it is difficult to set down any basic rules that will not immediately be called into question. It is like art: I know what I like, you know what you like, and there may be no area of agreement whatsoever. So, the following thoughts are very general and, no doubt, will be questioned by many.

It seems to me that there are good reasons for a boat to be attractive to the beholder. For one thing, anyone's life can be brightened by beautiful objects. A trip to an art gallery, or the view of a harbor full of handsome boats can provide a lift to the spirit. Furthermore, a boat which delights the eye of its owner will bring greater pleasure over the years than one with sturdy virtues but a plain appearance. If you love to look at your boat, you will find that you are willing to spend more time and money on her maintenance, thus lengthening her life. Look around at boats that are over 30 years old and still going strong—invariably they are handsome craft with a nearly universal appeal, and they have been well maintained by one or a series of doting owners. Finally, beauty in a boat has commercial value. When it is time to sell your boat, it is far easier to sell a beauty than a beast. Ask your broker.

When evaluating the aesthetic qualities of a design, try to visualize how the completed boat will look in three dimensions, when in the water and underway. Do all the various elements of the profile blend together well, or are there one or more discordant notes?

Let's examine the critical elements on a boat that are the most important from an aesthetic standpoint. They are the sheerline, the bow profile, cabin structure, rig, and freeboard. I place the sheerline first on the list because it is first in importance. Examine it closely and try to analyze what you like or don't like about it. Traditionally, sheerlines are highest at the bow, dropping to a low point two-thirds or three-quarters of the way to the stern, then rising again to a point somewhat lower than the bow height. Modern designers are departing from this tradition, and straight sheers, reversed sheers, and S-shaped, or powderhorn sheerlines (Figure 10) are all seen along the contemporary waterfront. While my own traditional

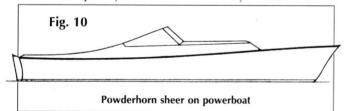

Fig. 10

Powderhorn sheer on powerboat

prejudices are pretty strong, occasionally I can admire a variant sheerline if it blends well with the other elements of the design to produce a pleasing effect. This is one of the keys to aesthetics in yacht design—the interaction of one element with another. There are not many fixed rules to be followed, and what excites one person may leave the next unmoved. But to my way of thinking, a sheer, to be pretty, should be a continuous sweep from end to end, fair and eye-sweet, and definitely higher at the bow than at the stern.

In Figure 11, "A" shows essentially the same boat as "B," with some slight changes in the critical lines. "A" shows what I think is a pretty profile. In "B," the relative height of the sheer at the ends has been changed, and the bow profile and the shape of the cabin have been altered. All these changes detract from the appearance of the boat.

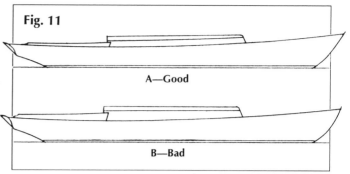

Fig. 11

A—Good

B—Bad

One interesting note about sheers is that while designers draw lovely sheers on paper, it is the builders who have to make them look right, and in most cases, the sheerline as drawn and lofted cannot be transferred exactly to the boat when built and still look correct. This is due to the perspective effects of the curved deckline in plan view. In most cases, the builder must put a little more upward swoop in the sheer at the ends, particularly at the bow, in order to avoid a droopy look or even a powderhorn appearance when the boat is built. The sheer at the stern of a double-ender is also a real challenge to a master carpenter. Some designers try to compensate for these perspective effects in their designed sheerlines, and you will see evidence of this on their lines drawings as a little extra curve upward near the bow and stern (Figure 12). Walter McInnis did this on many of the Eldredge–McInnis pow-

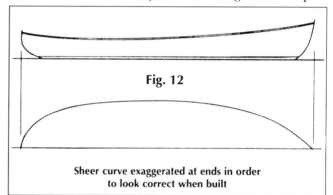

Fig. 12

Sheer curve exaggerated at ends in order to look correct when built

erboat designs, and rightly so, as the flared forward sections in most powerboats tend to exaggerate the powderhorn effect. The builder can only try to make the finished sheer look like the designer's lines plan. When you see a boat in the harbor whose sheerline makes you catch your breath, give a lot of credit to the builder, whose eye was experienced enough to accomplish this feat.

The bow profile, or shape of the stem, is the next most important line that catches one's eye. Again, there is an endless variety, from plumb and straight, through raked and convex-curved, to the double-S-curved clipper bow. All have their admirers, all can be very graceful, and all can be badly done.

There should be some correlation between bow and stern overhangs. Balanced overhangs generally look better than a combination of short and long overhangs.

Cabin profiles can do a great deal to improve or destroy the looks of a design. Long, low cabin sides with tumblehome and a pretty sheer to them can be a real visual attraction on a sailboat. For this reason, I think that a boat with a trunk cabin is handsomer than a flush-decked vessel. The placement and spacing of the cabin ports is also important. If the low cabin side described above happens to be executed in gleaming varnished wood, well, you can't go wrong. But so many cabins do go wrong—they are high and boxy, with funny-looking windows, and they often destroy the looks of an otherwise nice design. No amount of varnish can redeem them. The shape, size, and placement of the trim molding around the cabin will make a huge difference in the appearance of the boat. I cannot give you rules or standards for cabin design. Instead, study a lot of different cabins on the boats in your harbor, and make up your own set of standards.

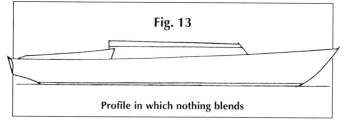

Fig. 13

Profile in which nothing blends

The rig is another major design feature that has a strong impact on the looks of the finished vessel. Again, this is a very subjective area, and I can only give you my own feelings about rigs and their relationship to appearance. I find the masthead rig to be less good-looking than the so-called fractional rigs, where the jibstay goes three-quarters or seven-eighths of the way to the top of the mast. Cutters, although their jibstay usually goes to the very top of the mast, are more visually interesting than sloops, because of their two headsails. Yawls and ketches are also more visually interesting than sloops. A tall rig will usually look better than a short, stumpy one, but rig height depends somewhat on the type of boat on which it is placed. A fast racer can have a tall, narrow rig to carry out the feeling of speed under sail, while a heavy-duty ocean cruiser would not look right with skinny, high-aspect-ratio sails. And here comes my pet peeve: Why are so many rigs designed with booms that are level or that even droop, with the clew lower than the tack? Well, the racers do it because the rating rules give them that little bit of extra sail area, free, without penalty. I suppose, for a flat-out racer, it is legitimate to use this extra area, but for everyone else, the appearance is so abominable that it should be outlawed. A nicely cocked-up boom adds so much to the looks that we should insist on a return to this style (see Figure 14). I think that sailmakers are partly at fault—they seem to build sails with a 90° corner at the tack as a matter of principle, even if the designer has shown it otherwise on his sail plan.

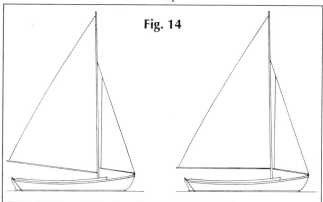

Fig. 14

Freeboard height is another element that has great impact on looks. Years ago, freeboard height was generally much lower than is drawn in present-day designs. Much of this increase can be traced to changes in the rating rules used to handicap boats for racing. Some of the increase has come about because more people are insist-

ing on having full headroom in small yachts. Another reason is that boats are generally of lighter displacement now, and have less hull volume below the waterline. The volume needed for decent accommodations, therefore, has to be above the waterline, and thus freeboards and cabins are higher. I still like the looks of the older, low-sided boats, with a sweeping sheer set off by a covestripe. But fashions change, and showing more topsides is now the normal thing.

Construction

To me, a wooden boat's construction plan is the most interesting drawing, and the most revealing one. It is usually the most detailed of the various sheets that make up a complete design, and is the one that has demanded the most time and thought from the designer. It is often possible to tell if the designer has had practical boatbuilding experience by studying his construction plan. The backbone members will have a simple, logical layout, and be of a size that is readily obtainable. The joints in the backbone will be engineered correctly, without bad cross-grain, the faying surfaces will be straight for ease in fitting, and the bolt plan will avoid conflicts with floor timbers, stopwaters, and shaftlogs. If the boat has steam-bent frames, the frame spacing will be a multiple of the station spacing, and the frames laid out so that they may be bent into place without conflict with the molds.

The other element which distinguishes the best construction plans from the poorer ones is a sense of proportion—each piece of the jigsaw puzzle that makes up the construction of a wooden boat will be correctly proportioned in relation to the whole. Planking thickness relates to frame size, deckbeam size relates to the beam of the boat and the spacing of the deck framing. The molded depth of the stem will provide sufficient back rabbet to ensure good fastening for the plank ends. All of these can be clues to the designer's experience with boat construction.

Some designers are better than others at producing "buildable" designs—designs in which ease of construction is an important parameter of the whole design process. The trick here is not so much to produce a design that is easy to construct, but rather to turn out a boat which is handsome, able, and fulfills the client's needs—and is also simple to build.

Construction plans have provided me with many happy hours of dreaming. I work through the sequence of steps in building the boat, puzzling over details here and there, and, by the end of an hour, I've imagined the tide high and the completed boat standing on her launching cradle, new paint gleaming, the brass all polished—a much more satisfying and less time-consuming process than the actual construction, which will take months, thousands of dollars, and a few sleepless nights.

I hope all of this will help you in looking at a set of boat plans. If you like boats and boat designs, there is nothing more fun and more instructive than studying plans by different designers. You will probably learn more than by taking a course in naval architecture. Make a clipping file of the designs that you like—I still have mine that I cut out of magazines more than 40 years ago, and still refer to it on occasion. When it is snowing outside and television palls, spread out some plans on the living-room floor. Give your imagination free rein, and you will be surprised at the voyages you can make.

Joel White designs and builds wooden boats in Brooklin, Maine. His Haven 12½ design will be found on pages 26 and 27 of this catalog.

Suggested Reading

The best way to learn boatbuilding is to start building a boat. Books and articles can help. They can keep you from entering the blind alleys that have trapped many of us, and they can show you several different paths to the same seaworthy results.

The following titles have been selected for their well-illustrated details and sound technical information. Further description of most of the books listed below, as well as information about back issues of *WoodenBoat* magazine, may be found in the current WoodenBoat *Catalog*, which is available on request from: WoodenBoat, P.O. Box 78, Brooklin, ME 04616.

Books

Birmingham, Richard. *Boat Building Techniques Illustrated*. Camden, ME: International Marine Publishing Co., 1984.

Bingham, Fred P. *Practical Yacht Joinery*. Camden, ME: International Marine Publishing Co., 1983.

Bray, Maynard. *How to Build the Haven 12 1/2 Footer*. Brooklin, ME: WoodenBoat Publications, Inc., 1987. (See Plan No. 75.)

British Forest Products Research Laboratory. *Woodbending Handbook*. London: Her Majesty's Stationery Office, 1970.

Bureau of Ships, U.S. Navy. *Wood: A Manual for Its Use as a Shipbuilding Material*. Kingston, MA: Teaparty Books, 1983.

Chapelle, Howard I. *Boatbuilding*. New York: W.W. Norton & Co., 1969.

Fine Woodworking Editors. *Fine Woodworking on Joinery*. Newtown, CT: The Taunton Press, 1985.

_____. *Fine Woodworking on Wood & How to Dry It*. Newtown, CT: The Taunton Press, 1986.

_____. *Fine Woodworking on Bending Wood*. Newtown, CT: The Taunton Press, 1985.

Frid, Tage. *Tage Frid Teaches Woodworking: Joinery, Tools and Techniques*. Newtown, CT: The Taunton Press, 1979.

The Gougeon Brothers. *The Gougeon Brothers on Boat Construction*. Fourth Edition. Bay City, MI: The Gougeon Brothers, 1985.

Hanna, Jay S. *The Shipcarver's Handbook*. Brooklin, ME: WoodenBoat Publications, Inc., 1988.

Hill, Tom. *Ultralight Boatbuilding*. Camden, ME: International Marine Publishing Co., 1987.

Hoadley, R. Bruce. *Understanding Wood*. Newtown, CT: The Taunton Press, 1980.

Howard-Williams, Jeremy. *Sails*. Fifth Edition. Clinton Corners, NY: John de Graff, 1983.

Kinney, Francis S. *Skene's Elements of Yacht Design*. New York: Dodd, Mead & Co., 1973.

Leather, John. *Clinker Boatbuilding*. London: Adlard Coles, Ltd., 1973.

McIntosh, David C. *How to Build a Wooden Boat*. Brooklin, ME: WoodenBoat Publications, Inc., 1987.

Miller, Conrad. *Your Boat's Electrical System*. New York: Hearst Books, 1981.

Nicolson, Ian. *Cold-Moulded and Strip-Planked Wood Boatbuilding*. London: Stanford Maritime, 1983.

Payson, Harold H. *Go Build Your Own Boat!* Thomaston, ME: Harold Payson, 1987.

_____. *Keeping the Cutting Edge: Setting and Sharpening Hand and Power Saws*. Brooklin, ME: WoodenBoat Publications, Inc., 1983.

Rabl, S.S. *Boatbuilding in Your Own Backyard*. Cambridge, MD: Cornell Maritime Press, 1958.

Simmons, Walter J. *Building Lapstrake Canoes*. Lincolnville, ME: Walter J. Simmons, 1981.

_____. *Finishing*. Lincolnville, ME: Walter J. Simmons, 1984.

_____. *Lapstrake Boatbuilding, Vol. 1*. Lincolnville, ME: Walter J. Simmons, 1983.

_____. *Lapstrake Boatbuilding, Vol. 2*. Lincolnville, ME: Walter J. Simmons, 1986.

Smith, Hervey Garrett. *Boat Carpentry*. New York: Van Nostrand Reinhold Co., 1965.

Spielman, Patrick. *Gluing & Clamping*. New York: Sterling Publishing Co., 1986.

Steward, Robert M. *Boatbuilding Manual*. Third Edition. Camden, ME: International Marine Publishing Co., 1987.

Toss, Brion. *The Rigger's Apprentice*. Camden, ME: International Marine Publishing Co, 1984.

Vaitses, Allan H. *Lofting*. Camden, ME: International Marine Publishing Co., 1980.

Watson, Aldren A. *Hand Tools: Their Ways and Workings*. New York: W.W. Norton & Co., 1982.

Witt, Glen L. and Ken Hankinson. *Boatbuilding with Plywood*. Bellflower, CA: Glen-L Marine, 1978.

Witt, Glen L. *How to Build Boat Trailers*. Bellflower, CA: Glen-L Marine, 1967.

WoodenBoat Eds. *Boatbuilding Woods: A Directory of Suppliers*. Brooklin, ME: WoodenBoat Publications Inc., 1987.

Articles in *WoodenBoat*

Adhesives

Buckley, Jennifer. "Holding Fast: Sonny Hodgdon on Glues." WB No. 59, p. 88.

Fraser, Aime´ Ontario. "Epoxy." Where, when, and how to use it. WB No. 84, p. 48.

Jagels, Richard. "Wood Technology: Joining Wood With Adhesives." WB No. 44, p. 133.

_____. "Wood Technology: Isocyanate Resins for Wood." WB No. 48, p. 123.

Pazereskis, John. "Icky, Sticky, Goo." WB No. 19, p. 46.

Schindler, Gerald. "Adhesives and the Boatbuilder." WB No. 4, p. 47.

Bedding Compounds

Wilson, Jon. "Keeping the Water Out From Under." The effective use of bedding compounds. WB No. 28, p. 76.

Boat Plans

Farmer, Weston. "Understanding a Boat Plan." WB No. 21, p. 30.

Boatbuilding (General Information)

Boatbuilding (How-to-Build Articles for Boats in This Catalog)

Caulking

Ordering Information:

Plans, books, and back issues listed on these pages may be ordered from WoodenBoat, P.O. Box 78, Brooklin, ME 04616. An order form has been included in this catalog for your convenience.

Due to fluctuations in price and inventory, we suggest that you check a recent issue of *WoodenBoat* magazine or the WoodenBoat Catalog for current cost and ordering information. Photocopies of articles from out-of-print *WoodenBoat* back issues are available for $2.50, including postage.

Please note that WoodenBoat's Ten-Year Index (issues 1–60) and Three-Year Supplement Index (issues 61–78) are highly recommended as more comprehensive and in-depth subject guides to all that *WoodenBoat* has published.

WoodenBoat Plans Policies

This catalog has been designed to inform and educate readers and prospective builders. While all information has been obtained from reliable sources and we believe it to be accurate, NO WARRANTY CAN BE MADE OR SHOULD BE IMPLIED with respect to this catalog's contents. Readers are urged to rely on their own good sense and personal experience when considering any design for reasons of performance or ease of construction.

While all care has been taken with each set of plans offered, the designer and WoodenBoat DISCLAIM ALL LIABILITY for loss or injury to property or person which might occur while using these boats, including loss due to careless handling or sailing of the boat under conditions beyond its reasonable limits. We also DISCLAIM ALL LIABILITY for boats built of inferior materials, to substandard workmanship, or to specifications or construction methods other than those suggested by the designer. Plans buyers who wish to modify a design IN ANY WAY are cautioned to do so only under the guidance of a competent naval architect.

Note: Plans are sold with the understanding that one boat only may be built from each set. If you wish to build more than one boat, please write for royalty terms. Plans may not be reproduced in any form, or by electronic or mechanical means, without permission. Plans can be accepted for return only in exceptional circumstances and with our prior permission. In such cases, we must charge a restocking fee of $5.00. Plans cannot be shipped C.O.D.

*General Notes on Designs

Performance section:

WoodenBoat's comments concerning the type of waters a boat is suitable for, as well as a vessel's intended capacity (number of persons), are based on the boat being used by experienced people in favorable wind and sea conditions. Owners are advised to check U.S. Coast Guard capacity regulations, where applicable.

Building Data section:

Information regarding alternative construction methods for a design means only that the hull shape would lend itself to these alternative methods. Unless otherwise noted, plans *do not* include details for modified construction, and builders must rely on their own resources.

It should also be noted that Weight/Displacement figures provided under "Particulars" are estimated for small unballasted craft without people or gear aboard.

How to Order

PHONE ORDERS
CALL TOLL-FREE
1-800-225-5205
Mon.-Fri. 8am-11pm est.

Please fill out the order form before you call. It is your record of the order. Use the info below to figure shipping costs. We will ask for your 4-digit catalog code, which is located after your address on the right side of your order form.

VISA AND MASTERCARD ARE WELCOME
Your credit card will not be charged until your items are shipped.

OR WRITE: WoodenBoat Catalog
P.O.Box 78
Brooklin, Maine 04616

Payments must be made in U.S. dollars payable thru a U.S. bank. We process & ship most orders within <u>3 working days.</u>

CUSTOMER SERVICE
If you have any questions about a product or an order, please call our customer service department toll-free, 1-800-225-5205.

RETURN POLICY
We want you to be pleased with every item you receive. If you are not, just return it for a courteous replacement, refund or credit. (Sorry, there is a $5.00 restocking fee with the return of plans.)

OUR GUARANTEE
We have gone to great lengths to offer top-quality, specialized and hard-to-find products. Your satisfaction is our main concern. If you are not 100% satisfied, notify us and we will replace, refund or credit promptly.

SHIPPING & HANDLING
Please select the appropriate area shipping charge according to destination & delivery method & include that charge in the box on your order form.

OTHER MERCHANDISE
To order books, back issues, or the index, please check a recent issue of WoodenBoat magazine or the WoodenBoat catalog for current cost and ordering information.

WoodenBoat Catalog
P.O. Box 78 • Brooklin, ME 04616

WoodenBoat Merchandise

TOLL-FREE HOURS: 8A.M.-11P.M. EST.,M-F (10A.M.-5P.M. ON SATS., OCT. THRU DEC.)

 1-800-225-5205 OR IN MAINE & CANADA **207-359-4652**

FAX in US: 207–359–8920 FAX overseas: 010–0–207–359–8920
Please FAX your completed order form, including VISA or MASTERCARD information.

OR WRITE US:
WoodenBoat Catalog P.O. Box 78, Brooklin, Maine 04616

NAME (SOLD TO) _____

ADDRESS _____

_____

CITY _____ STATE____ ZIP_____

SHIP TO (if different than above) _____

ADDRESS _____

_____

CITY _____ STATE____ ZIP_____

YOUR DAY TEL# _____   CATALOG CODE **V2PL**

OUR SHIPPING & HANDLING CHARGES
Please select the appropriate area shipping charge according to destination & delivery method & include that charge in the box below. We process and ship most orders within THREE working days.

Within the U.S.A.		To Mexico & Canada		All Overseas	
Eastern Time Zone	$1.75	Surface Mail	$ 7.50	Surface Mail	$ 8.00
Central, Mtn., Pac.Zones, Hawaii & Alaska	$3.50	Airmail	$11.00	Airmail	$32.00
or for Priority Shipping to <u>all</u> zones, send	$7.00				

For orders outside the U.S. with 8 or more items, we may need to charge shipping/handling on a per order basis. Please feel free to call or write for a quote.

QTY	PRODUCT #	PRODUCT	PRICE EACH	TOTAL

Payment must be in U.S. dollars payable through a U.S. bank. We accept ▭ or ▭ or Check or Money Orders.	
CARD NUMBER	▯▯▯▯▯▯▯▯▯▯▯▯▯▯
EXPIRES: MONTH/YR	
SIGNATURE OF CARDHOLDER	

TOTAL MERCHANDISE	
Maine Residents Add 5% Tax	
REGULAR S. & H. Charge From Chart Above OR...	
PRIORITY S. & H. Charge From Above	
For each Product # with a "W" add 50¢ ($1 overseas)	
WOODENBOAT SUBS.	
TOTAL (at last!)	

WoodenBoat's Guarantee...
Satisfaction or Your Money Back!